The Selected Poetry of
JAROSLAV SEIFERT

The Selected Poetry of
JAROSLAV SEIFERT

Translated from the Czech by
Ewald Osers

Edited and with Additional Translations by
George Gibian

ANDRE DEUTSCH

First published in Great Britain 1986 by
André Deutsch Limited
105 Great Russell Street London WC1B 3JL

ISBN 0 233 9797 9

Printed in Great Britain by
St Edmundsbury Press, Bury St Edmunds, Suffolk

ACKNOWLEDGMENTS

A few of the poems in this volume have appeared in *The Plague Column*, Terra Nova Editions, London & Boston, 1979, and in *An Umbrella from Piccadilly*, London Magazine Editions, London, 1983. In the 1985 edition of *2 plus 2*, Mylabris Press, Lausanne, the following poems appeared: Apple Tree with Cobweb Strings, The Wax Candle, Dialogue, Funeral Under My Window, A Hundred Times Nothing, Song of the Native Land, Reluctant Whisper of Kissed Lips, Robed in Light, Song of the Sweepings.

CONTENTS

While this book was being printed, Jaroslav Seifert died in Prague, on January 10, 1986.

The editor of this volume met with Seifert for the last time in his hospital room in Vinohrady, Prague. He had been hospitalized for some weeks, suffering from viral pneumonia. A few days later he was released and returned to his own home.

During the editor's last visit with him, he was alert, vivacious, and as gracious as always. He displayed intense interest in many subjects — in everthing going on around him, near and far. He asked questions about life in the United States, family, friends, politics, Gorbachev, the Geneva Summit conference, and he related amusing incidents and mishaps which had occurred to him — and to friends of his — in Prague and Paris, during his youth and in recent days. He asked about the progress in the publication of the present volume of his selected works in English and talked about a translation of his poems into Catalan, which had been published in Barcelona, and a Spanish edition of his reminiscences, which, he said, had reportedly become a bestseller in Spain, to his surprise.

To make changes in the body of the book at this stage — changing the present to the past tense, for example — would have meant a delay in the publication. Publishers, translator and editor all felt that Seifert's work would be best served by avoiding such a delay and by going ahead with the book as it was planned during the poet's life.

With Jaroslav Seifert's death, the Czech nation lost the last member of the remarkable group of poets to whom it had given birth in the first third of the twentieth century.

GEORGE GIBIAN

INTRODUCTION
The Lyrical Voice of Czechoslovakia

When the Nobel Prize for literature was awarded to Jaroslav Seifert in October 1984, the Czechs, who know Seifert's works well and love them, were proud and delighted, but outside of Czechoslovakia, readers were puzzled. They were curious about Seifert's poetry and its background, and wondered who Seifert was and whether he deserved the prize.

The present volume of English translations of selected poems by Seifert, and of passages from his prose memoirs, is intended to answer these questions.

I

In 1984, Seifert, who was born in 1901, was the last survivor of a galaxy of Czech poets, most of whom had come into prominence in the third decade of this century and had been closely associated with one another. Seifert often pays tribute to his late friends and fellow poets, men he loved and admired and each of whom he depicts with one or two brilliant strokes of his pen.

Seifert might be called the "Grand Old Man" of modern Czech poetry. He may also be thought of as the embodiment of a literary type which has died out in most Western countries — the national poet. Poetry is much more widely read and appreciated by Czechs than by the English-speaking public. Although there are only about ten million Czechs, the number of copies published — and sold — of works by Czech poets is frequently several times larger than that of American poets in the United States, which has a population twenty times greater. Or, to put it another way, perhaps fifty times as many books of poetry are bought by Czechs as by Americans.

In Czechoslovakia poetry is regarded as a normal, everyday activity. The names of famous poets, such as Seifert and his colleagues, are household words. Their works are widely quoted and discussed; their funerals are mass occasions. They are respected by the "people" as well as by the elite; their support is solicited and their hostility feared by the rulers. When Seifert was seriously ill, crowds assembled outside his house and stood in silence, in a spontaneous show of concern and respect.

Czech poets are expected to express the deep feelings of the nation in matters of everyday life — love, nature, and death — and also to speak out about major public issues. The nation awaits their poetic comments about such national events as the death of President Masaryk in 1937, the occupation of the country by the Germans in 1939, and the successive landmarks of Czechoslovak history since the liberation in 1945.

Behind Seifert's poetry lies the long history of Czech literature, which had several periods of special prominence: the Middle Ages, the Seventeenth Century, the Romantic period, and the late Nineteenth Century. In the first half of the Twentieth Century, lyrical poetry dominated the Czech literary scene. A whole pleiad of poets wrote outstanding works, which, if written in a world language such as English, French, or German, might have become internationally famous. There were some outstanding novels and plays (those of Čapek and Hašek are well known abroad, while Vančura's are known only in his own country), but it was into poetry that the main energy of Czech literature flowed. (After 1960, the critical, rational genre of the novel appears to have grown stronger than it ever was before.)

Modern Czech poetry is marked by the bold use of freely associative imagery and by its intense emotionality. It is difficult or sometimes impossible to translate when it relies heavily on the resources of the sounds of the Czech language (play on the patterns of vowels and consonants, lengths of vowels, stress), and has remained almost unknown outside of Czechoslovakia.

II

A brief survey of Seifert's life and literary activities may be helpful towards a better understanding and appreciation of the translations of his works.

Jaroslav Seifert was born on September 23, 1901, in Prague, in a working-class neighbourhood called Žižkov. Throughout his life, he liked to recall his childhood there, in a part of town marked by a strong proletarian flavour, with many tenements, railroad tracks, balconies, taverns, and even its own dialect or slang, comparable to the Cockney dialect of London. The tough, swaggering manner-isms of his Žižkov youth stayed with Seifert for a long time. The poet František Halas, later Seifert's closest friend, described their first encounter, in the Moravian capital of Brno:

2

Seifert arrives. I cannot forget our meeting one noon, in July. Across the street I see someone walking with a sailor's stride. A warm scarf instead of a [detachable] collar, a pipe; he spits continually. In those days a poet inevitably looked like that. I walk towards him instinctively: "You are Seifert?" "You are from Žižkov?" I wasn't from Žižkov, but he was Seifert.[1]

Seifert's mother was Catholic and his father an atheist and socialist. Seifert felt warmly towards both of them.[2] Although his parents were poor, they were not destitute. Seifert was able to study in a "gymnasium", an academic secondary school attended by only a minority of the boys his age. He did not graduate, but left the gymnasium early and started working as a journalist and devoting himself to literature. Later he was to describe his beginnings as a poet with gentle self-mockery.[3]

With World War I (1914-1918) not yet over and the future Czechoslovakia still a province of Austria-Hungary, the teen-aged Seifert wrote his first poems. His earliest poetry, often highly didactic, showed sympathy for the proletarian cause and for anarchism. When Czechoslovakia became independent in October 1918, Seifert associated with the left wing of the Social Democratic party, and became one of the first members of the Communist Party when it was organized in 1921.

Seifert's first volume of poetry, *Town in Tears*, is usually considered the most "proletarian" work of all Czech poetry, but Seifert the poet prevailed over the man of politics even then. Love held its own in his poetry against fervour for revolutionary action. Revolutionaries whose priorities placed public commitment above private concerns disapproved of such passages in Seifert's poetry as the following:

> Love is something huge
> You'll find out
> If there were revolution in the whole wide world
> Still somewhere on green grass
> Lovers would have time to hold hands
> and lean their heads towards one another.

Seifert thought of the Revolution primarily as a source of future happiness for the poor, a people's carnival, rather than organized political action and violence; love was stronger in him than hate.[4]

Some of his early poems were already outstanding in their utterly unpretentious simplicity and directness:

I have a window
a spring day floats in it
like a boat with a pink flag on a river,
I have a dog
it has human eyes,
I have a blue note book
and in it
thirty-three beautiful names of girls.
. . .
And so I won't forget
I have an empty box of shoe polish,
a sad, dried out flowerpot on the window sill,
a flower in my buttonhole
and tears in my heart.

Some of Seifert's modernist friends (Teige, Neumann) played a role in weaning him away from his earliest poetic style of "workers' poetry", and in bringing him closer to more avant-garde artistic circles. In 1920 Seifert was one of the founders of a modernist group of artists and writers called *Devětsil*. The name is that of a medicinal herb or wildflower, and means etymologically "Nine Strengths", or "Nine Forces".

In the 1920s, Seifert's life and works were closely linked to this group and to a related artistic movement called "Poetism". Both *Devětsil* and Poetism were key avant-garde movements in Czech culture. The ambitious, boastful, highflown aspirations of *Devětsil* are suggested in a brief passage in its manifesto:

Before all creative human work today stands the immense task of rebuilding the world anew. . . . Poets and thinkers stand shoulder to shoulder with revolutionary soldiers. Their task is the same. . . . There is only one road towards tomorrow. . . . The art of yesterday, whether we call it Cubism, Futurism, Orphism, or Expressionism, considered that "the thing in itself" was beautiful and that was enough.

Devětsil urged going beyond "the thing in itself", in a proletarian, Communist direction. Poetism regarded life itself as an art form and aspired to include all the arts under its aegis.

Its utopian aim was to fuse life with the arts, so that, in the remote future, art would become life and life art — in whatever sense one might interpret this high but vague goal. Its leading theoretician was Seifert's friend Karel Teige (1900-1951).

The 1920s were for Seifert and his friends a heady time of youthful, provocative, sometimes exhibitionist, always exuberant immersion in poetry, journalism, art, and political discussion. This close-knit group of young men and women, who were constantly meeting in cafés and bars to debate art and life, produced remarkable works of art and literature. They felt (and they were) innovative, daring, and radical.

"Poetism" meant a loosening of connections. Metaphors and ideas could play more freely; poetry was to be a game of the imagination with words. Continuities and clarity of references became blurred, or disrupted altogether (as in the work of e.e. cummings):

> cigarette smoke
> climbs
> a tourist in the Alps
> sun and depth
> over a steep cliff
> the summit of Mont Blanc
> acrobatics of roses
> from the clouds
> rise to the stars
> the pillows of boredom
> drink them
> Poetry

The movement was also saturated by the atmosphere of its physical setting: the lyrical, moody environment of the ancient city of Prague, with its river, bridges, parks, architectural monuments, churches, and other landmarks. Seifert's poetry has always been particularly rich in Prague themes.

Seifert wrote for a variety of newspapers and reviews, several of them Communist ones. After periods of work as a reporter for a Communist newspaper in Prague and another in Brno, the capital of the province of Moravia, Seifert worked in a Communist bookshop and publishing house in Prague, and in the late 1920s edited a Communist illustrated magazine.

Seifert's first book of poems, *Town in Tears*, was published in 1921. Throughout the twenties, he continued to publish his own poetry, as well as translations, including those of the Russian Symbolist poet Alexander Blok and of the French poets Paul Verlaine, Guillaume Apollinaire, and others. Seifert made a long journey, with his friend Teige, through Vienna, to North Italy,

Marseilles, and Paris, and revisited Paris twice more. He also travelled in the Soviet Union in 1925 and 1928.

In the late 1920s, Seifert was beginning to sense that the close-knit circle of *Devětsil* had outlived some of its meaning for him and his friends. In 1929, together with eight other prominent Czech Communist writers, he signed a letter opposing the line which the new leadership of the Communist Party had adopted regarding culture. He was expelled from the Party (unlike some of his fellow signatories, he never rejoined), as well as from *Devětsil*. He then worked briefly as reporter and editor on various daily and periodical publications, such as the Socialist Democratic daily *Právo lidu*. He wrote many volumes of poetry, and compiled and edited the works of Czech classics of the nineteenth century (those of the poet Hálek, and of Neruda, the Czech writer whose name the Chilean poet was to adopt as a *nom de plume*).

Seifert's books of poetry in 1929, 1933, and 1936 developed further his characteristic use of euphony. His poems were often densely compressed, had a song-like quality, and emphasized the resources of sound (intonation, rhymes, assonances, and alliterations), qualities difficult to translate. Poems which illustrate his delicate, evanescent, lyrical art include "The Wax Candle" (p.40 below), and "You Have Skin Pale Like a Snowdrop":

> You have skin pale like a snowdrop,
> but a mouth fragrant like a rose.
> The words of love are monotonous,
> what shall I do with them now
> that I am waiting for your reply
> and in confusion hurrying for it.
> You have skin pale like a snowdrop,
> but a mouth fragrant like a rose.
>
> Only don't deceive me in the end,
> but let the fear that screens your eyes
> vanish quickly, please look —
> like the snow that fell last year.
> You have skin pale like a snowdrop,
> but a mouth fragrant like a rose.

Another example is "Venus's Hands":

The slow adventurer
sat down on the shore
and tells the wave
his vain stories;
they are only
a handful of wind
on the palm of the hand,
the death of pearls in wine,
the fear of not dying.

But that is not
his true calling.

When the rooster crows,
the dew freezes
and plucks the rose blossoms,
he says to himself:
how cruel it is
to tear the poor rose,
its petals are rose
like the nails at the toes.

But that is not
his true calling.

To watch the birth of beauty,
to weep its destruction,
to wait for the blossoms
of next spring
near flowing waters,
which again deafen
the eternal hesitation,
to put one's head in the palms
of the hands of Venus of Milo,

Oh, alas, that is
his true calling.

Around 1930, Seifert's poetry reached the peak in its song-like virtuosity. He used regular stanzaic forms, ingenious rhymes, and frequent refrains. The favourite subjects of his polished poems of this period were the beauty and tenderness of women and the fleetingness of love.

In 1937, his volume entitled *Eight Days* expressed the sadness felt by most Czechs at the death of the first president, Thomas Masaryk, a philosopher and statesman who symbolized the democratic and independent spirit of the First Czechoslovak Republic. *Put Out the Lights* (1938), his next cycle of poems, was a poetic journal of the days first of excitement and later of gloom when Hitler's Germany menaced and then annexed Czechoslovakia piecemeal. In this period the Czechoslovak Army, mobilized and prepared for the defense of the country with the enthusiastic backing of the people, was ordered by President Beneš, after the Munich Conference in September 1938, to withdraw and abandon the national borders.

In March 1939 the remainder of Czechoslovakia was occupied by the Nazi armies. Seifert published three volumes of poetry during the German occupation and World War II, in which he attempted to strengthen the nation's resolve to survive with dignity. They expressed love for his homeland, for Prague, and for the Czech language, and with them he won the widest recognition of the Czech public. It was between 1939 and 1945 that he reached the status of unofficial national poet. His own perilous experiences during the last days of the German occupation in May 1945 are vivdly described by him in his memoirs (pp.171–175 below).

With the liberation of the country in May 1945, Seifert again became very active in journalism. After a Communist government took over in February 1948, he found himself under attack, vilified in the press by some of the adherents of the new regime and of "socialistic realism". He withdrew from public life. A minor critic attacked him as alien, bourgeois, and un-Communist in an article under a heading which later became notorious, "Not Our Voice".

His publications were limited to editing the works of various Czech authors and to translating (outstanding was his translation of the biblical *Song of Songs*).

After 1954, however, as a cultural thaw started, selections from his past works began to be published, along with some new poetry. In 1956, during the period of liberalization in the Soviet Union, he spoke from the platform at the Second Congress of the Union of Czechoslovak Writers: "May we be truly the conscience of our people. Believe me, I am afraid we have not been that for quite a few years; we have not beeen the conscience of the masses, the conscience of millions; we have not even been the conscience of ourselves . . . If somebody else keeps silent about the truth, it can be a tactical manœuvre. If a writer is silent about the truth, he is lying."

Seifert demanded that the transgressions of the Stalinist era be acknowledged and rectified, and the victims of injustice compensated. Thus the poet who in the 1920s and '30s was known for his fragile love lyrics now became a spokesman for civic consciousness and public commitment.

Seifert's "courageously fair" speech made a deep impression on the audience, as did the poet's physical appearance at the time. Seifert walked with difficulty, leaning on a cane. When he sat, however, he looked like a cliff: immovable, unbudgeable, solid, firm. An eyewitness wrote later: "We felt relief that he was with us . . . a poet, spread out wide, his crutches leaning against the table, tangible proof of the genius of the nation, the sole glory of the powerless."[5] Seifert's verses,

> Still evil rises
> Up the bone marrow of humanity
> Bespat with blood like the stairs from a dentist's,

were also unforgettable.

After the silence of a decade of serious illness, Seifert emerged with a surprising new poetic manner. In *Concert on the Island*, 1965, and later works, he gave up much of his song-like intonations, rhyme, and metaphor, for the sake of simple, declarative, unadorned free verse.

During the "Prague Spring" days, in 1967, he received a prize from the Czechoslovak Writers' Publishing House, and in the same year was named National Artist of Czechoslovakia.

In August 1968, armed intervention by the Soviets in Czechoslovakia spurred Seifert, who had been seriously ill, to rise from his sickbed, call for a taxi, and go to the building of the Union of Writers. The writers present elected him acting chairman of the independent Union of Writers. A year later, this union was dissolved. Isolated, sick, Seifert went on writing. His poems were typed and distributed in hundreds of copies by individual readers. He lived in his suburban house in Břevnov (Prague), helped anyone who called on him, and wrote reminiscences of his long life as a poet. The reminiscences are a veritable encyclopaedia of

9

Prague's cultural life. Seifert mingles in them details of his private life with accounts of his sixty years of association with Czech writers, artists, and journalists. Ten passages excerpted from these reminiscences are translated in this volume.

Between 1968 and 1975 only selections from his old works were published inside Czechoslovakia, but a few of his new poems were published in Czech, in periodicals produced abroad.

On August 16, 1976, in an open letter to the German novelist Heinrich Böll, Seifert asked for support for a Czech musical group which found itself under attack, and this letter was followed by the drafting and promulgation of Charter 77, of which Seifert was one of the original signers.

With the passage of years, Seifert's new works were again published inside Czechoslovakia. English translations by Ewald Osers, Lyn Coffin, and others appeared in the United Kingdom and in the United States. An anthology of his poetry from various periods was published in the Czech original, in Toronto, and another in Prague. When his memoirs, *All the Beauties of the World*, were published in Czech in Toronto, a parallel edition, under the same title, and with minor deletions and alterations, was published in Prague.

His illness required him to be hospitalized repeatedly. His poetry dealt frequently with death (and love):

> When I collapsed in pain
> death wet its finger with saliva
> to put out
> the little red flame of my blood,
> she who was closest to me came,
> knelt beside me
>   and bent low
> to breathe sweet breaths into my lungs —
>   long kisses as if for a drowned man.
> He who was already leaving
>   reopened his eyes
> to clutch furiously with his hands
>   her shoulders leaning over him and her hair.
> Perhaps it is possible to live without love
> but to die without love
> Is desperation.
> My life ran its course quickly.

It was too short
for all my long yearnings,
they were endless.
Before I knew it
the end of my life had drawn near.
Death will soon kick my door
        and come in.
At that moment
from terror and fright
I will hold my breath
and forget to breathe in again.

After Seifert's Nobel Prize award, in October 1984, the eyes of
the world were upon him. Television crews and newspaper
reporters descended on him. Interviews of varying degrees of
sophistication and accuracy were published all over the world. In
1985, he was able to leave the hospital and return to his house, in
excellent spirits, continuing to write poetry.

III

All his life, Seifert has been enraptured by the beauty of the
physical world. Modestly and unpretentiously, he infects his
readers with his love of life and his joyfulness.

He is a poet of the world of the senses, not of transcendence,
Angst, fear, or trembling. He is not a learned or an intellectual
poet, but a concrete, popular one. Not theories and abstractions,
but the sensuous and emotional values of life draw his attention
and praise.

As one Czech critic, Jan Vladislav, has put it, the baroque
palaces of Prague speak to Seifert of love and of the tangible
softness of a woman's skin. The courtyards, alleyways, gates,
doorways, and gardens of Prague are to him akin to the other pole
of attraction recurring throughout his work — the desire of the
human race for harmony and contentment.

His kind-hearted, gentle acceptance of the enjoyment of life is a
very un-Calvinist one, that of a person unburdened by guilt.
Seifert's sunny poetic personality is rare in the twentieth century.
It has much in common with Mozart's. His heliotropic inclination
towards grateful enjoyment of life is not Pollyanna-like, however.
It rests on two important bases: compassion for the suffering of
others and a gentle irony.

Seifert's concern for those in pain is most marked in his preoccupation with the sufferings of the Jews during World War II. Seifert is surely one of the most outstanding Gentile poets to have expressed a sense of horror and pathos at the Nazi extermination of Jews. Again and again he returns to this topic, sometimes as his major theme (for example in his poem "A Song at the End", about little Hendele, a Czech Jewish girl killed in a Nazi camp, and the chapter in his memoirs about the lonely survivor of the concentration camps, Elsa, [p.176 below], and at other times in incidental references. The fate of the Jews is never far from Seifert's awareness. His references cover a wide chronological range from the Old Testament, through the Old Jewish Cemetery in Prague, to our own times. He does not dwell only on Jewish suffering, but also on the capacity for joy and love embedded in Jewish traditions. He translated the *Song of Songs* of Solomon, and he frequently refers to the beauty and the smiles of Jewish women.

Irony, particularly in his self-deprecating thrusts, is another quality of Seifert's poetry. It is characteristic of him that, as he relates in his memoirs, when he was face to face with death, threatened with immediate execution by the Germans in May 1945, he did not think of religious or metaphysical subjects or the terrors of the universe, but wondered what the people living in the apartments nearby were cooking for lunch and also suddenly remembered the indecent drawing of a woman on the wall of a public latrine which used to fascinate him when he was a small boy. He is without false pride, without the need to keep up appearances, to strike an impressive figure. He tells us repeatedly how unheroic he is.

Just as Seifert is never self-important or pompous, so his poetry shows a determination not to allow eulogies of joy and beauty to be based on self-deception. Irreverence and scepticism are always close at hand. Seifert is ever ready to puncture balloons, especially his own. His lighthearted "Rooster's Sonnet", for instance, illustrates this:

Rooster, I was awakened by your song
and, as if I had forgotten those who were sleeping,
I sang out loud, and picked a bunch of grapes —
we were just riding through a vineyard.

How nicely one can live in this world of ours;
you resemble me, it seems.

12

We both sing, flapping our wings,
and both remain down on the ground.

Your metal image on the ridge of the roof
turns with the wind as I do.
Our dreams go on and on; our fleas keep jumping.

No, I'm not weeping for love;
crocodile tears are like chicken feed
that I picked by the sea in an idle moment.

The speaker does not forget the "fleas" which are always present
and "jumping". Elsewhere Seifert enjoys quoting the jab of a
friend who explained that Seifert's many trips from a small village
to a coffeehouse in a larger town were motivated not by his love of
coffee, but by his nostalgia for the smell of the sewers of Prague
(p.162 below). Prague, Seifert's beloved town of sculptures, churches, music and beautiful women, is for him also associated with
the unforgettable odour of a sewage system. When in his reminiscences Seifert recalls the prostitute whose naked breasts fascinated
him when he was sixteen, and forever marked him with love for
women's beauty, he also emphasizes that she lived in a brothel
guarded by a sordid old woman, where a fat rat dragged something
nasty across the threshold. Seifert insists on acknowledging all
sides of life.

A readiness to undercut his own flights of emotion and aspira-
tion comes naturally to Seifert, but his basic orientation is not a
debunking one. He may laugh at his adolescent romantic dreams
and sentimentalities, but what he calls his youthful "limping" and
"stumbling" after women's beautiful hair and breasts, and his
boyish deification of poetry did remain the twin poles of his life.
He glories in them and pursues them, even after irony has done all
its work.

Seifert's tone is usually that of a close friend. He speaks as if he
and his reader were comrades sharing a common culture and set of
attitudes towards life. Such parenthetical phrases as "of course",
"as we know", are frequent in Seifert's poems and memoirs. His
poetry is very allusive: his references to Czech culture range from
the anniversaries of historic events to the sculptures and other
architectural landmarks of Prague. The emotional resonances these
cause in Czech readers may be lost on non-Czechs. He speaks as if

one could assume everyone will know where Mozart lived when he was in Prague, and what he composed there, or who Mácha was and even what his sweetheart's name was. Foreign readers (and also Czech readers of a younger generation) may need to have various passages annotated and explained. It is for this reason that a Glossary identifying persons and place names is included in this volume, as well as some additional explanatory footnotes.

Seifert shows his awareness of the fact that the times have changed. When, for example, he speaks of his veneration of women, he also tells us he realizes that the romantic worship of women is now old-fashioned — yet he proceeds to relate how he used to feel and still feels, despite the vagaries of fashion.

The criteria for the selection of poems included in this anthology are threefold: intrinsic quality, representativeness, and translatability. We have made an effort to choose poems from various periods of Seifert's work and to illustrate his various modes. We have also given preference to poems (and passages from the prose reminiscences) which deal with universal themes and we have tended to avoid those which depend heavily on special Czech circumstances and interests.

The poems of Seifert's early and middle periods often depended so heavily on effects of sound that they lose much of their quality in translation or are altogether untranslatable. For this reason, while some poems of these periods are included, the bulk of the volume consists of poems written since the 1950s, the time when his poetry became more translatable into foreign languages.

The poetic traditions behind Seifert's works derive mainly from two lines of literary ancestry: major Czech poets (the Nineteenth Century Romantic poet Mácha and others widely read in Czechoslovakia, although little known abroad, such as Erben, Neruda, Vrchlický); and the French masters, some of whom Seifert translated, Verlaine, Baudelaire, Cendrars, Supervielle, Apollinaire, and others.

Seifert's poetry evolved from a rather brief initial "proletarian" phase, through the long "modernist" period, to the simple, transparent, "conversational" phase of the last two decades. However, similar preoccupations have remained evident throughout his life. His major themes from beginning to end have been love and the beauty of women, Prague and the fate of the Czech nation, and the sensuous pleasures and joys of life. Themes of only slightly less importance have been death, sorrow and pain; Paris and French culture; and Mozart.

In the 1960s, when Seifert turned to unrhymed poetry which is intimate, almost epistolary, eroticism continued to be an important theme; but suffering, pain, death, and melancholy assumed more prominent roles.

The seeming ordinariness of some of his recent poems is deceptive. Within their prose-like narratives, there is a strange tension. Seifert suddenly leaps out with poignant words or lines, which are all the more powerful for the contrast with the light touch of the passages surrounding them. We settle into the expectancy of reading a plain, even banal text, and then the poem startles us with something original which, retroactively, transforms our perception of the preceding passages. We see them as inventive, skewed, and demanding.

Seifert is difficult to translate for the English reader because much of his poetry plays on the sound resources of the Czech language. Not only is Seifert a genius at finding surprising, original rhymes, but he mingles meters and rhythms with patterns of vowels and consonants, assonances, internal rhymes, and half-rhymes. Particularly untranslatable are his harmonies based on long vowels, which in Czech are independent of stress and carry phonological meaning (unlike those in English or Russian).

However, the chief qualities of his poetry can be conveyed in translation, and they enjoy universal human appeal. To recapitulate, his poetry, particularly in the last decades, is understated, simple, unrhetorical, and unpretentious. Another important quality is its .sensuality. Seifert's eroticism and hedonism are not exhibitionistic, but rather accepting and natural. A concern with suffering, pathos, melancholy, and with death itself (see p.109, "The Mistess of the Poets"), always present, becomes still more pronounced in the second half of his literary life.

Seifert can sing, and particularly in the poems of the 1920s and 1930s, he often rises to great heights of lyricism. There is great charm and even magic in his poetry. Occasionally he achieves deep pathos, with a poignancy all the more powerful for its rarity. This is especially true of his poems about Prague and the killing of Jews in World War II.

IV

When I visited Seifert in his house in the Břevnov suburb of Prague, in February 1985, he proved to be lively, alert, mischievously witty, and eager to ask questions. Mindful of his past illnesses and hospitalizations, I started to take my leave several times, so that my presence would not exhaust him too much, but each time he insisted on continuing to talk and to pour more white wine for his company and himself.

He is a natural raconteur. The chronological scope of the stories he told reached from his childhood to the day before our conversation. With schoolboy glee he recounted how, the previous afternoon, a scientist sent by the Swedish Academy had paid him a courtesy call in connection with his Nobel Prize. One of the things the Swedish scientist had asked him, Seifert said, was which kiss had been the best of his whole life.

Seifert was obviously very pleased with the answer he had given. He told the visitor that two kisses tied for first place. One was when he first kissed the woman who later became his wife. The second took place after a friend telephoned him, a long time ago, to say that the chamber containing the jewels of the Czech kings was being unlocked, and that if Seifert hurried, he could come and see them. Seifert rushed to the Cathedral where he touched the crown of the Czech kings with his own hands and then leaned over and kissed it. That was the second of the two best kisses of his life. The Swedish dignitary liked his answer very much, Seifert said with a twinkle in his eye: "Swedes like that kind of thing."

Seifert took great interest in the translations of his poems being published abroad and asked many questions about them. He was particularly pleased that a volume of his poetry translated into Catalan had been published in Barcelona by a Czech woman living in Spain, Monika Zgustová. Seifert obviously feels a special sympathy, or fraternal collegiality with Catalans, a people who like the Czechs, are comparatively few in number.

Seifert complained that some interviewers from Western nations — journalists from both magazines and TV networks — had been inaccurate, had invented answers he had never given, and had proved to be tactless and politically unsophisticated.

He recalled with special warmth his friend Roman Jakobson, the late linguist and literary scholar, and pointed with pride to a photograph standing on his desk, which showed Jakobson gesticulating, with a hand raised typically high. Seifert said this was the last photograph taken before Jakobson's death.

With regard to his own poetry, Seifert stressed that translators and readers must not forget that although the lines of his recent poems may be unrhymed, there are many internal rhymes and other sound patterns within his verses, which should not be ignored.

Seifert's apartment is in a house with a garden behind a fence with a small gate, in a quiet suburban street high on the ridge of a hill in Břevnov, one of Prague's "small villa" residential sections. Present were his daughter Jana, an energetic, businesslike, lively person; his son, a quiet, self-effacing scientist; and two Czech visitors — a poet and translator, and a journalist. Seifert's wife, who suffers from hearing difficulties, walked into the room several times for a few minutes, but did not participate in the conversation. Seifert and his daughter took the initiative in steering the conversation in various directions.

Seifert himself sat at his desk, drank tea and white wine, and was every inch the cordial host. His study is full of objects connected with his poetry and his particular affections — statuary, including heads of angels and madonnas, works of Czech poets, Czech folk art, pictures of wildflowers, and a photograph of the legendary hill Říp, on which the progenitor of the Czech people stopped and decided to settle in what is now Czechoslovakia.

On another occasion, to another interviewer, Seifert made comments which summarize eloquently his basic views on the connections between poetry, sensuality, and freedom, and which can appropriately conclude our introduction to his works:

My origins are proletarian, and I thought of myself for a long time as a proletarian poet. But as one grows older, one discovers different values and different worlds. For me, this meant that I discovered sensuality. . . . All language can be thought of as an effort to achieve freedom, to feel the joy and the sensuality of freedom. What we seek in language is the freedom to be able to express one's most intimate thoughts. This is the basis of all freedom. In social life, it ultimately assumes the form of political freedom. . . . When I write, I make an effort not to lie: that's all. If one cannot say the truth, one must not lie, but keep silent. . . .

It is poetry which has the subtlety needed for us to be able to describe our experience of the world. The fact that we speak by means of our human voice causes poetry to touch us personally, directly, so that we feel our whole being is involved.[6]

* * * * * * * * * * *

I want to express my warmest gratitude to the Rockefeller Foundation, which enabled me to have leisure and quiet to make the final revisions of this volume at its Study Center in the Villa Serbelloni in Bellagio on Lake Como; to Mrs Diane Williams, who patiently and speedily retyped successive versions of the translations, introduction, glossary, and notes; and to Professor Karen Brazell, for many excellent suggestions on how to improve the English texts.

As for the series of personal meetings with Mr Seifert in Prague in the course of the year 1985, they were a delight and an inspiration. It was a privilege to be a witness to his invariably gracious manner and to his poetic genius which manifests itself strongly also in his casual conversations.

George Gibian

Cornell University
Ithaca, New York

The Poetry of
JAROSLAV SEIFERT
Translated by Ewald Osers

TOWN IN TEARS

A sharply-drawn picture of suffering
is the town,
and it is the one great object that stands in your sight.
Reader, you open a plain and unpretentious book —
and here my song takes flight.

Although I look
upon the glory of the town, my heart it cannot overpower;
its majesty and greatness do not dazzle me;
I shall return to the mysterious embrace
of star, of wood and brook, of field and flower.
But so long as one of my brothers
is suffering, I cannot be happy
and, bitterly revolting against all
injustice, I shall long
continue, amid the suffocating smoke, to lean against a factory wall
and sing my song.

Yet strange to me is the street, I've found.
Swiftly it flies like an arrow to conquer the world.
Into the rhythm of my blood they will never tune in,
        the running belts and the wheels
with which my hands and the hands of thousands are bound,
so that, whatever a man's heart feels
he must not and cannot embrace his mate.

Yet were I to flee to the wood and the deer, to the flower and the
    brook,
such sorrow would weigh my heart down
that, without turning to look
at all the beauty and quiet and passion,
I should go back to the town,
the town that welcomes one in its ice-cold fashion,
where the nightingale ceases to sing and the pine-wood loses its
    smell,
where not only man is enslaved,
but the flower, the bird, the horse and the humble dog as well.

Gentle reader, as you read these lines,
reflect for a moment and note this down;
the sharply-drawn picture you scan
is the town.
Why, man feels just like a flower:
Don't pluck him, don't break him, don't tread on him!

SINFUL CITY

The city of factory owners, boxers, millionaires,
the city of inventors and of engineers,
the city of generals, merchants and patriotic poets
with its black sins has exceeded the bounds of God's wrath:
God was enraged.
A hundred times he'd threatened vengeance on the town,
a rain of sulphur, fire, thunderbolts hurled down,
and a hundred times he'd taken pity.
For he always remembered what once he had promised:
that even for two just men he'd not destroy his city,
and a god's promise should retain its power:

just then two lovers walked across the park,
breathing the scent of hawthorn shrubs in flower.

A SONG ABOUT GIRLS

Across the city flows a mighty river,
seven bridges bestride it;
along the embankment walk a thousand pretty girls
and no two are alike.

From heart to heart you go to warm your hands
in love's great warming flame;
along the embankment walk a thousand pretty girls
and they're all the same.

RED-HOT FRUIT

To love poets
the vanishing fauna of Yellowstone Park
    And yet we love poetry
    poetry
    the eternal waterfall

Long-range guns were shelling Paris
    Poets in steel helmets
But why count those who died of unhappy love?
    Goodbye Paris!

    We sailed round America
and fish with diamond eyes
died in the screws of the steamer
    what hurts most
    is one's memory

    Negro lyres
    and the smell of hot air
the red-hot fruit of chandeliers only ripens towards midnight
    and Monsieur Blaise Cendrars
lost a hand in the war

    Sacred birds
on slender legs like shadows
rock the fate of worlds
    Carthage is dead
And the wind plays in the sugar cane
    a thousand clarinets

Meanwhile on brittle parallels of the globe
    History
    century-old ivy is twining
I'm dying of thirst Mademoiselle Muguet
    and you won't tell me
how the wine must have tasted in Carthage

A star was struck by lightning
        and it's raining
The water's surfaces
        swirl like taut drum skins
Revolution in Russia
        the fall of the Bastille
and the poet Mayakovsky is dead

        But poetry
        a honeyed moon dripping sweet juices
        into the flowers' calixes

HONEYMOON

If it were not for all those foolish kisses
we'd not be taking honeymoon trips to the sea —
but if it weren't for honeymoon trips
what use then all those *wagon-lits*?

Perpetual fear of railway station bells,
ah *wagon-lits*, honeymoon sleeping cars,
all wedded happiness is brittle glass,
a honeyed moon stands in a sky of stars.

My love, look at the Alpine peaks outside,
we'll let the window down, we'll smell the amaranth,
the sugary white of snowdrops, lilies, snow —
behind the *wagon-lit*'s the *wagon-restaurant*.

Ah *wagons-restaurants*, cars for a honeymoon,
to stay in them forever and to sup
with knife and fork on dreams that end too soon.
HANDLE WITH CARE! GLASS FRAGILE! THIS SIDE UP!

And one more day and then another night,
two marvellous nights, two marvellous days like these.
Where is my Bradshaw, that poetic book,
oh but the beauty of my *wagons-lits*!

Oh *wagons-restaurants* and *wagons-lits*!

Oh honeymoons!

PHILOSOPHY

Remember the wise philosophers:
Life is but a moment.
And yet whenever we waited for our girlfriends
it was eternity.

*   *   *

THE FAN

To hide a girl's blushes,
provocative eyes, deep sighs,
finally wrinkles and a smile become wry.

A butterfly alighting on her breasts,
palette of loves gone by
with the colours of faded memories.

MOSCOW

The minuet has long ceased to be danced,
the harp has long lost its last audience.
The display cases in the old palace
are tombstones of the dead.

There were battlefields here,
the Kremlin's bloodstained wall still shows its teeth.
Bear witness for us, you who are dead,
buried in silks.

Cups without wine,
flags dipped over the past,
a sword that recalls
from whose hand it dropped.

Rotten rings, a mildewy diadem,
a corsage that's fragrant still,
the disintegrating robes of dead tsarinas
with an eyeless mask, the look of death and damnation.

The orb, symbol of power, lying on the ground,
an apple worm-eaten and rotten.
All's over, all is over under the golden domes,
death is guarding history's graveyard

Suits of armour, empty like golden nutshells
on carpets of unparalleled design,
and *empire* carriages drive back into the past
without horses, without lights, without occupants.

APPLE TREE WITH COBWEB STRINGS

Deep-red apples
bowed down the royal trunk like a harp,
autumn fitted it with cobweb strings,
ring and sing,
      my player!

We are not from the land where oranges grow,
where round Ionian columns climb the vine
that's sweeter than
      the lips of Roman women;
ours but the apple tree, fiercely bowed down
      by age and fruit.

Beneath it sits a man
      who's seen all this:
Parisian nights, Italian noon,
      above the Kremlin a cold moon,
and has come home to reminisce.

      A tune that sings
a calm and quiet song that could be played
upon these cobweb strings
      sounds in my ear.

And where is beauty found?
      On mountains, cities, seas,
where do the trains take you in search of peace,
to heal still smarting wounds?
Where?

      And women's eyes,
their breasts, whose rise and fall
would rock your head in rich erotic dream,
      do they not tempt you?
A voice that's redolent of distance calls you:
      Your land is small!

And you stay mute
when that seductive voice speaks to the vagrant
in you? Midday is gone,
I pick an apple from the ancient tree,
inhale its fragrance.

To be alone and far
from women's laughter and from women's tears,
to be at home, alone,
with the familiar tree-song in your ears.

Why, the vain beauty of some foolish women
isn't worth an apple.

PANORAMA

The stag is retreating, the smoke of its antlers is rising
through the fern's foliage, listen to the star,
but softly, only softly.

Plates full of fruit, nights full of stars,
I'd like to hand you this bronze bowl
and be a barber.

Oh hairdressers,
tired hands gliding down smooth hair,
a comb is dropped, the sculptor drops his chisel
and in the mirror eyes have turned to ice.

It's night already. Are you asleep?
Shatter the softness of your eiderdowns!
The midnight hour. Electric lamps.
Dark, light, dark, half-light
and behold:

The comb of mountains combs the hair of the sky
and stars are falling fast like golden lice.

DANCE OF THE GIRLS' CHEMISES

A dozen girls' chemises
drying on a line,
floral lace at the breast
like rose windows in a Gothic cathedral.

Lord,
shield Thou me from all evil.

A dozen girls' chemises,
that's love,
innocent girls' games on a sunlit lawn,
the thirteenth, a man's shirt,
that's marriage,
ending in adultery and a pistol shot.

The wind that's streaming through the chemises,
that's love,
our earth embraced by its sweet breezes:
a dozen airy bodies.

Those dozen girls made of light air
are dancing on the green lawn,
gently the wind is modelling their bodies,
breasts, hips, a dimple on the belly there —
open fast, oh my eyes.

Not wishing to disturb their dance
I softly slipped under the chemises' knees,
and when any of them dropped
I greedily inhaled it through my teeth
and bit its breast.

Love,
which we inhale and feed on,
disenchanted,
love that our dreams are keyed on,
love,

that dogs our rise and fall:
nothing
yet the sum of all.

In our all-electric age
bars not christenings are the rage
and love is pumped into our tyres.
My sinful Magdalen, don't cry.
Romantic love has spent its fires.

Faith, hope and motorbikes.

SONG

We wave a handkerchief
on parting
every day something is ending,
something beautiful's ending.

The carrier pigeon beats the air
returning;
with hope or without hope
we're always returning.

Go dry your tears
and smile with eyes still smarting,
every day something is starting,
something beautiful's starting.

PRAGUE

Above the elephantine blankets of flower-beds
a Gothic cactus blooms with royal skulls
and in the cavities of melancholy organs,
        in the clusters of tin pipes,
old melodies are rotting.

Cannon-balls like seeds of wars
were scattered by the wind.

Night towers over all
and through the box-trees of evergreen cupolas
the foolish emperor tiptoes away
into the magic gardens of his retorts
and in the halcyon air of rose-red evenings
rings out the tinkle of the glass foliage
as it is touched by the alchemists' fingers
as if by the wind.

The telescopes have gone blind from the horror of the universe
and the fantastic eyes of the astronauts
have been sucked out by death.

And while the Moon was laying eggs in the clouds,
new stars were hatching feverishly like birds
migrating from blacker regions,
singing the songs of human destinies —
but there is no one
who can understand them.

Listen to the fanfares of silence,
on carpets threadbare like ancient shrouds
we are moving towards an invisible future

and His Majesty dust
settles lightly on the abandoned throne.

WET PICTURE

Those beautiful days
when the city resembles a die, a fan and a bird song
or a scallop shell on the seashore
— goodbye, goodbye, pretty girls,
we met today
and will not ever meet again.

The beautiful Sundays
when the city resembles a football, a card and an ocarina
or a swinging bell
— in the sunny street
the shadows of passers-by were kissing
and people walked away, total strangers.

Those beautiful evenings
when the city resembles a rose, a chessboard, a violin
or a crying girl
—we played dominoes,
black-dotted dominoes with the thin girls in the bar,
watching their knees,

which were emaciated
like two skulls with the silk crowns of their garters
in the desperate kingdom of love.

NOVEMBER 1918
(In memoriam Guillaume Apollinaire)

It was in autumn. Foreign troops
had occupied the vineyard slopes,
emplaced their guns among the vines, like nests,
and aimed them at the Gioconda's breasts.

We saw a sad impoverished land,
soldiers without legs or hands
but not without a spark of hope,
the fortress gates were swinging open.

A scent-filled autumn sky: below it
a city with an ailing poet,
a window to the evening sun.
Here is a helmet, sword and gun.

The city, true, is not where I was born,
its rivers flow along without concern,
but once below a bridge there I had wept:
a pipe, a pen, a ring are all I kept.

The gargoyles up by the cathedral's rafters
vomit the city's dirt into the gutters,
their heads bent forward from the cornice toppings
and fouled and spattered by the pigeons' droppings.

The bells ring out, the bronze notes fall,
but this time without hope at all,
a funeral cortège must pass
down the boulevards of Montparnasse.

The ripples on the river told the birds,
the birds flew up to tell the clouds
and sang the news up in the skies:
the stars that evening did not rise.

And Paris, as it stood, City of Light,
shrouded itself in deepest, blackest night.

PARTING

So foolish are the hearts of many women,
of beautiful and ugly ones alike,
their footprints are not easy to distinguish
in the sands of your memory.

But what you minded most
at our final parting
was that in my poor rags
— but was it not the costume of a beggar? —
you couldn't see your tears as in a suit of armour.

Goodbye, you swarm of flies
which buzzed into my dreams,
goodbye, my quiet evenings and
my cigarette case with the engraved rosette!

Opening the door I heard the screams
of angels hurtling down to hell.

THE WAX CANDLE
for A.M. Píša

Born of the buzzing hives
and of the smell of flowers,
honey's little sister,
honey-bathed for hours

till from that fragrant bath
lifted by angel's hands —
and in the month of love
bees wove its garment strands.

When a dead man collapses
at its feet like one at rest
on a train of black shadows
then it will comb its crest

and down its waxen body
will run a red-hot tear:
Come with me, dear departed,
your bed is waiting here.

A HUNDRED TIMES NOTHING

Maybe once more I shall be driven mad
by your smile
          and on my pillow gently as a feather
will settle Mother Grief and Girl Friend Love,
always the two together.

Maybe once more I shall be driven mad
by the cornet's tune
and my hair will smell of gunpowder
as I walk like one who's dropped from the Moon.

Maybe once more I shall be driven mad
by a kiss:
          like a flame in a reluctant lantern I'll begin
to tremble
as it touches my skin.

But that will only be the wind on my lips
and in vain will I try
to catch its incorporeal dress
as it flits by.

DIALOGUE

[She]
Was it my forehead or my lips you kissed?
I do not know
— all I heard was your enchanting voice
and dark mist
veiled the wonder of my startled eyes.

[He]
Hastily I kissed you on your forehead,
for I felt my senses go
from the fragrance of your flowing breath
but I still don't know:

— all I heard was your enchanting voice
and dark mist
veiled the wonder of my startled eyes.
Was it my forehead or my lips you kissed?

FUNERAL UNDER MY WINDOW

I complain to the wind, our life's but a minute,
horses, turn back,
if only the horses could turn back:
give us back our time, once more to begin it!

If only the clock striking backwards could bring
us the moments we wasted, frittering,
if the machine, running in reverse,
undid the noose of the suicide,
if only the moon which set yesterday
returned once more to the sky today,
if only we knew how to weep again
over our trivial sorrows!

I complain to the wind – hear its howl and its din –
if only the wind could turn,
returning the mask to the dead skin,
the mask which at the point of death
flew off the face with its last breath
and which the wind now sweeps and batters –
to let us kiss it once again
before it's borne away and shatters
among the foliage, in the drops of rain.

SPANISH VINEYARDS

Once more the earth is sending up its juices
into the low vines on these stony lands.
And the young plants, if they aren't shot to pieces,
are gladly holding out their leafy hands

like beggars hoping for a sun-warmed coin.
Oh charming villages which give renown
and name to those sweet juices swelling out
the grapes that bow the slender branches down.

It's April now and drops of crimson blood
are spattered over simple smock and hand.
Ah, Spanish grapes, who will be here to pick you
one day when all this fighting's at an end?

SALUTE TO THE MADRID BARRICADES

Covered in quicklime in his native soil
Garcia Lorca, warrior and poet,
lies crouching in the dugout of his grave
without a rifle, lyre, ammunition.
The rug of days on which the Moors are dancing
is woven now from pools of tears and blood,
and across Alpine glaciers, Pyrenean heights,
from the ancient stairway leading to the Castle,
a poet's speaking to him,
a poet still alive,
with his clenched fist sends to that distant grave
a gentle kiss,
the kind that poets have for one another.

Not for murder
but for days of peace
sounds the sweet song
and that soft play, the play of words and rhymes
that we have sought
under our lovers' hearts and under trees in blossom,
to shape a verse
as sonorous and as beautiful
as ringing bells and speech on plain folk's lips.

But when the pen turned into a rifle
who did not flee?

A bayonet, too, can write on human skin,
its letters burning like the crimson leaves
through which I'm wading at this difficult hour.

Yet one thing I do know, dead friend:
along the boulevards of Madrid
workers will march again and they will sing
your songs, dear poet,
when they've hung up the rifles they now lean on,

when they have hung them up in gratitude
as do the lame in Lourdes
their now no longer needed crutches.

＊　＊　＊

SONG OF THE NATIVE LAND

Beautiful as on a jug a painted flower
is the land that bore you, gave you life,
beautiful as on a jug a painted flower,
sweeter than a loaf from fresh-ground flour
into which you've deeply sunk your knife.

Countless times disheartened, disappointed,
always newly you return to it,
countless times disheartened, disappointed,
to this land so rich and sun-anointed,
poor like springtime in a gravel-pit.

Beautiful as on a jug a painted flower,
heavy as our guilt that will not go away
— never can its memory decay.
At the end, at our final hour
we shall slumber in its bitter clay.

ROBED IN LIGHT

I.

As I was walking in the fading light —
Prague seemed more beautiful than Rome to me —
I was afraid that from this dream I might
never awake, that I might never see
the stars that, when the daylight comes again,
beneath their folded wings the gargoyles hide —
the gargoyles standing, as on guard, beside
the cornice of St Vitus' ancient fane.

One morning in the early hours, too late
to go to bed — the dawn was drawing near —
I stood before the still unopened gate
of the great church, but would not knock for fear,
as a poor pilgrim, on a winter morn,
finding it shut, will stand beside a door;
I wished to see the gargoyles just before
they greet the stars returning home at dawn.

Instead I saw a tomb and went to view
the statue on it — all alone was I;
Like a wrecked ship appeared the dead man's shoe;
its toe was pointing upwards to the sky.
And as I looked a flickering candle flung
strange shadows on the tomb from head to heel;
it was as though I heard the spinning-wheel
and peasants' songs amid the vineyards sung.

The grapes are in the royal garment's weave,
in grey, as early-morning human breath,
four ladies sleeping in the Gothic nave
are carrying the dead man on their breasts.
Remember me to Karlštejn's woods, their pines
descending gently to the sunlit plains.
Remember me to Karlštejn's walls again
and to the hillsides clad in verdant vines!

From his tomb he raised above the pillars
(sprouting, so it seemed, out of his palms)
a blanched human skull; behold, a lover's
hands created for caress and charms
touched it and the touch lent it endurance
through a nation's song whose lips had cracked,
gave it strength, it was a secret pact
that was left of its inheritance.

Why, its lips from thirst were bound to numb —
ceaselessly it slept upon its sword —
through the ages rang the ancient hymn,
ardent song of safety and accord.
And the Saint, obscured now by the shapes
of wings of angels and the shield of prayer,
broke white bread among his country's poor
and with his own feet trod the firm white grapes.

In confusion I regard this majesty,
press into the beggars' shade nearby,
I'm not here to weep among the amethysts,
I have long forgotten how to cry.
The lace edge of the altarcloth was torn,
the music stand had spilled a few sheets:
through the long nave rang steps of heavy boots,
clicking darkly on the floor's mosaic.

TO PRAGUE

So much I loved you, though with words alone,
my lovely city, when your cloak was thrown
wide open to reveal your lilac charms;
much more was said by those who carried arms.

Yes, they were plentiful, our daily tears
as, streaming down, they salted our bread.
The voices of our dead rang in our ears,
the just, reproachful voices of our dead.

Upon the pavement of our streets they lay,
and I shall always, even unto my grave,
feel shame I was not with them on that day.
You gallant city, bravest of the brave,
eternally enshrined in mankind's story:

That day enhanced your beauty and your glory.

AT THE TOMB OF THE CZECH KINGS

Shame in my heart, I stand among the agates —
those jewels of our land!
The faithful sword whose resting place is near
was not to hand!

Like dew besprinkling leaves and blossoms
while dormant still in bud,
the sword, the lance, the chain-mail gauntlet
were always splashed with blood.

To pray? But let the sword be drawn
and flash the while we pray!
Only the women may have empty hands now.
And not even they!

The clock moves on, though time is running slow
on our Renaissance spire.
The hand of history's written on the wall
new signs of fire.

But there's dried blood on it, a spark is kindled:
the chained will disobey.
Only the women may have empty hands now.
And not even they!

To fold our hands in miserable prayer,
wait for a better day?
Only the children may have empty hands now.
And not even they!

WHEN IN THE HISTORY BOOKS ...

When in the history books
one day you read our story,
when neither fame nor sorrow
seem what they once had been,
when summer comes again
and girls in all their glory
reveal their charms in
veils of crepe-de-chine,

and one of them, embarrassed,
hands lying on her dress,
will tremble oh so slightly
as you bend down with fire,
inhale her fragrant breath
sweet as wild raspberries
and kiss her on her lips,
then on her chin and lower,

remember: to be carefree
was also my desire,
make love to girls, be happy,
believe that life was sweet.
Alas, my rose-red mantle
was ripped by sharp barbed wire
and our nights re-echoed
the tread of marching feet.

When in the history books
one day you read our story:
about a land that flourished,
of hail and floods in spring,
maybe you'll catch the sound
of drum-rolls funerary
and from our epoch's depth
will cruel laughter ring.

HOW PAINFUL I WOULD FIND IT ...

How painful I would find it
        to leave these well-loved walls
for ever! There were moments
when I believed life was impossible
without their shadows, which reach far beyond
our short lives.

The compass rose no longer urges me
        towards unknown distant places
and its rays perhaps have died for me.

        Yet the green trees
with their long-striding roots
are keeping pace with me here.

LOVERS, THOSE EVENING PILGRIMS

Lovers, those evening pilgrims,
walk from darkness into darkness
    to an empty bench
and wake the birds.

Only the rats, which nest with the swan
on the pond's bank under the willow branches,
sometimes alarm them.

Keyholes are glittering in the sky,
and when a cloud covers them
somebody's hand is on the door-knob
and the eye which had hoped to see a mystery
gazes in vain.

— I wouldn't mind opening that door,
except I don't know which,
and then I fear what I might find.

By now that pair were falling down together
in a close embrace,
and in that state of weightlessness
were reeling in spasms of wonderment.

The mists are dancing, wearing wreaths
of daisies, rust, droppings of birds,
    their swirling cloaks
still red from the extinguished evening sky.

But those two, lips to lips,
are still beyond this world,
    beyond the door of heaven.

— When you start falling hold on to me tight
and hang on to your scarf!

SOMETIMES WE ARE TIED DOWN ...

Sometimes we are tied down by memories
and there are no scissors that could cut
through those tough threads.
     Or cords!

You see the bridge there by the House of Artists?
     A few steps before that bridge
gendarmes shot a worker dead
who'd walked in front of me.

I was only twenty at the time,
     but whenever I pass the spot
the memory comes back to me.
It takes me by the hand and together we walk
to the little gate of the Jewish cemetery,
through which I had been running
from their rifles.

The years moved on with unsure, tottering step
and I with them.
     Years flying
till time stood still.

IF ONE COULD TELL ONE'S HEART

If one could tell one's heart:
    don't rush!
If one could bid it: Burn!
The flame is dying.
    Only a slipper now,
only a hand,
    only a thimble now
before the key turns, opening the door
through which we pass with tears
for that terrible beauty
    called Life.
Don't feel ashamed. Lord Jesus also wept.
Last night the stars shone so brilliantly.

But why should a single blade speak of
    itself
when there is grass?
    I do apologize,
I only want a few words.

When I collapsed with pain
and death already was licking its finger
to snuff out
the small red flame of blood,
came the one woman who was closest to me,
knelt down beside me
    and bent low
to breathe, with her long kisses,
her breath into my lungs, as to a drowned man.

And he, already leaving
    opened his eyes again
and desperately with his hands hung on
to her shoulders and hair.
Maybe it's possible to live without love —
but to die without it
    is sheer despair.

Just one more little leaf,
     just one more grain,
only a pinhead's worth!
So I can for just a little longer stagger
in the mild sunshine of womanhood,
which draws us close and leads us away,
     seeks and passes,
urges and restrains,
     strikes down and raises up,
binds and loosens,
     caresses and kills,
wing and anchor
     fetter and ray,
rose and claw to the end.

RELUCTANT WHISPERS OF KISSED LIPS

Reluctant whispers of kissed lips
    which are smiling Yes —
I've long since ceased to hear them.
    Nor do they belong to me.
But I'd still love to find words
    kneaded from
    bread dough
or the fragrance of lime-trees.
Yet the bread's become mouldy
    and the fragrance bitter.

And all round me the words sneak on tiptoe
and stifle me
    when I try to catch them.
I cannot kill them
    but they're killing me.
And blows of curses crash against my door.
If I forced them to dance for me
they'd stay mute.
    And they hobble.

Yet I know very well
that a poet must always say more
than is hidden in the roar of words.
And that is poetry.
Else he could not with his verses lever out
a bud from honeyed veils
or force a shiver
    to run down your spine
as he strips down the truth.

SONG OF THE SWEEPINGS

What's left of all those beautiful moments?
    Lustre of eyes,
    a drop of fragrance,
    some sighs on the lapel
    breath on a window-pane
    a pinch of tears,
    a scraping of grief.

And after that, believe me, hardly anything.
    A handful of cigarette smoke,
    some hurried smiles,
    a few words
    now swirling in the corner
    like sweepings
    stirred by the wind.

And then — I'm glad I remembered —
    three snow-flakes.

    And that is all.

         *   *   *

And now don't smile!
    Heaven, hell, paradise —
these are not mysteries but just a children's game,
    nothing more terrible,
with children hopscotching into the square
where their pebble has landed.
When rain was in the air the sewers stank.

I too played all these games
    but snow and rain
then soaked my heaven.
Why did they sprinkle our streets?

The semicircle at the top was paradise,
where hell was I can't now remember.
 Yet hell was there.
But in the raindrops
the world would glisten
and snow was even more beautiful than now.

Once on that pavement I found a woman
who'd been killed.
 It was Advent, it was early morning,
when in the churches they would sing Rorate
and from somewhere wafted the smell of pine needles.

In her fingers she clutched an empty handbag
 and a little further on
lay a powder compact with its mirror broken.

Rorate coeli! Whoever had torn off her clothes
had ripped her blouse.
 Rorate coeli desuper!
Cold rain was falling
and the arc lamp rocked
 its wet shadow.

Then they covered the corpse with a tarpaulin.

 *   *   *

With thumping heart,
 oh, how often,
I walked past dirty curtains in the windows,
breathlessly waiting
 for some hand to draw them back.
As for a woman's face,
 I never saw one then,
 stirring reality was fleeing from me.

No, it was I who fled before it
and my eyes shrank
          in shamed confusion.
And all my yearnings were afraid.
What I so hungrily had wished to see
          I suddenly caught sight of.

I did not then suspect
how passion can disrobe
when it wants to be evil.
The blood was still there the next day.
And that was that hell.

A SONG AT THE END

Listen: about little Hendele.
She came back to me yesterday
and she was twenty-four already.
And was as beautiful as Shulamite.

She wore a light-grey squirrel fur
and a pert little cap
and round her neck she'd tied a scarf
the colour of pale smoke.

Hendele, how pretty you look!
I thought that you were dead
and meanwhile you have grown more beautiful.
I am glad you've come!

How wrong you are, dear friend!
I've been dead twenty years,
and very well you know it.
I've only come to meet you.

HALLEY'S COMET

I saw nothing at that moment,
        nothing but strangers' backs,
but heads under their hats moved sharply.
The street was crowded.

I'd have liked to scramble up that blank wall
by my fingernails,
        the way addicts of ether try to do,
but just then my hand was seized by
        a woman's hand,
I took a few steps
and before me opened those depths
we call the heavens.

The spires of the Cathedral down on the horizon
        looked as if cut out
from matt silver foil,
but high above them the stars were drowning.

There it is! See it now?
        Yes, I see it!
In trails of sparks which would not die
the star was vanishing without return.

It was a spring night, sweet and mild,
        after mid-May,
the soft air was laden with perfumes
and I inhaled it
        together with the star dust.

Once when in summer I had tried to smell
        — and only furtively —
the scent of some tall lilies
—they used to sell them in our market-place
in kitchen jugs —
people would laugh at me.
For on my face was golden pollen dust.

ST GEORGE'S BASILICA

If in the white Basilica of St George
fire broke out,
        which God forbid,
its walls after the flames would be rose-coloured.
Perhaps even its twin towers: Adam and Eve.
Eve is the slimmer one, as is usual with women,
though that is only an insignificant glory
        of their sex.
The fiery heat will make the limestone blush.

Just as young girls do
after their first kiss.

PROLOGUE

To be a poet is no easy task:

He spots a warbler in the woods
flying above its nest
and he can't stop himself from thinking
— O wicked ecstasy! —
of the warm tousled dimple
in his girl's armpit.

Yet he walks on into the wood
because he can hear voices
and everything around is softly trembling.
And what d'you know?
      Quite close he'll see
the downy crotches of young women,
first one, another,
receding into the dim distance,
leaving behind them longing.
Oh no,
      they are just leaves and flowers,
the pinkish trunks of the tall spruces
glistening after the rain.
They are most beautiful during the day
and then at night.
      But it's not me.

Once, in the past, the poet raised his voice
and blood crowed loud.
Men rushed to take up arms
and women did not hesitate to cut
their honey-hued and dark-red hair
for bowstrings.
They're more elastic than our nylon strings.

Today girls wear their hair too short
and that is why they now put gauze
on human wounds
        and hasten to the injured
to bear their blood-stained heads
upon the stretchers of their breasts.

Unless the tyrant falls
        — and that's hereditary too —
the poet is condemned to silence
and the sharp-edged hand of prison bars
will shut his mouth with iron claws.
But he will scream his verses through the bars
while the burners of books
get down to work.
        But that's not me!

Sometimes he'll desperately clash his words together
to produce some certainty —
but there's no certainty in our world.
And vainly does he fling his fiery words
far, even beyond death,
to dangle some mute mystery,
to lighten the darkness that lies motionless
on this mass grave
        and merely clings
to miserable bones,
spattered with verdigris from the lighter
they overlooked in the executed man's trouser pocket.
        But that's not me!

*   *   *

I never told anyone about it
but I was there.
        The night birds will testify to it,
the barn owls and the nightjars,
        whose sight is penetrating even in the dark.
Children are not believed,
        it's said they lie,
but I was there, I was there at the time!

Midnight had gone,
the stars were shining as if crying
and I was shivering with cold on those last rungs
high up, right at the top
        of Jacob's ladder.
It rested firmly on the ground
    and leaned against a cloud.

But half-way up, above a drift of stars,
I froze in terror:
        a gilded harp
was flying upside down, from nowhere into nowhere,
circling the earth all round.
Some of its strings were broken
and it looked like the severed wing
        from an angel's back.

No doubt it happened in some cosmic storm
when the fine stardust blows
into the vast cornfields.
        The butterflies of spring
start in alarm
from the wet stones.

What happened when I'd climbed the ladder
right to the top
I'll tell you in a moment
        The memory of it sets my heart aflame.

Out of its pitch-black silk
        — it was that dark —
a lovely star emerged
and rose upon its silent trajectory,
as large as the full moon
        seen from a window.
It shone like milk
        with just a little colour from the blossom
that had fallen into it.

Such beauty I'd seen once before.
It had been my first secret.
And yet it was no sin: she was unaware of it.
As she undressed
        her head was turned away.
She has long been dead.

When I came down again
        to the larks' nests
and the cockerels crowed their warnings of daybreak
I saw yet another thing that time!
What was it then?
        A ray from Alcyone.
And down below an ancient carriage creaked,
its wheels crushing the windfalls, while on the horizon
stood Říp Hill.

                    ✻   ✻   ✻

Once I followed my father
to an open-air meeting.
        They sang a different tune:
There'll be an end to emperors and kings
and cast off your chains!

I would have cast them off
except I didn't feel their weight yet
but I admired the Phrygian cap,
the drum on its broad strap
and the bullet-torn flags.

And the next day I hurried to the Castle
up the most beautiful stairway in the world
and with a thrill gazed down upon the city.

To have a lute, to have the skill to play it,
I could have burst then into joyful song,
those days when from the blue upon the sky
and from the smiles
          which were not mine
I wove my dreams. Yes, they were childish
and quite ridiculous.

Then I expunged it all and started out afresh
in the same way.

I don't remember now
          which way I drifted
but one brief moment stands before my mind.

                    *   *   *

Through a half-open door I saw a hall
with people dancing.
The drapes inside the windows were all festive
as though a canopy held over youth.
Young girls in white, young girls in pink,
young men in elegant dark suits
were whirling round delightful expectations.

Enchantment sometimes makes you catch your breath.
And then abruptly someone slammed the door.

ONCE ONLY . . .

Once only did I see
the sun so blood-red.
          And never again.
Ominously it sank towards the horizon
and it seemed as if
someone had kicked apart the gates of hell.
I asked at the observatory
and now I know why.

Hell we all know, it's everywhere
and walks upon two legs.
          But paradise?
It may well be that paradise is only
a smile
          we have long waited for,
and lips
          whispering our name.
And then that brief vertiginous moment
when we're allowed to forget
that hell exists.

If you call poetry a song
— and people often do —
then I've sung all my life.
And I marched with those who had nothing,
who lived from hand to mouth.
I was one of them.

I sang of their sufferings,
        their faith, their hopes,
and I lived with them through whatever
they had to live through. Through their anguish,
weakness and fear and courage
and poverty's grief.
And their blood, whenever it flowed,
spattered me.

Always it flowed in plenty
in this land of sweet rivers, grass and butterflies
and passionate women.
Of women, too, I sang.
Blinded by love
        I staggered through my life,
tripping over dropped blossoms
or a cathedral step.

PLACE OF PILGRIMAGE

After a long journey we awoke
in the cathedral's cloisters, where men slept
on the bare floor.
There were no buses in those days,
only trams and the train,
and on a pilgrimage one went on foot.

We were awakened by the bells. They boomed
from square-set towers.
Under their clangour trembled not only the church
but the dew on the stalks
as though somewhere quite close above our heads
some elephants were trampling on the clouds
in a morning dance.

A few yards from us the women were dressing.
Thus did I catch a glimpse
for only a second or two
of the nakedness of female bodies
as hands raised skirts above heads.

But at that moment someone clamped
his hand upon my mouth
so that I could not even let out my breath.
And I groped for the wall.

A moment later all were kneeling
before the golden reliquary
hailing each other with their songs.
I sang with them.
But I was hailing something different,
yes and a thousand times,
gripped by first knowledge.

The singing quickly bore my head away
out of the church.

In the Bible the Evangelist Luke
writes in his Gospel,
Chapter One Verse Twenty-six
and following:

And the winged messenger flew in by the window
into the virgin's chamber,
as softly as the barn-owl flies by night,
and hovered in the air before the maiden
a foot above the ground,
imperceptibly beating his wings.
He spoke in Hebrew about David's throne.

She only dropped her eyes in surprise
and whispered: Amen
and her nut-brown hair
fell from her forehead on her prie-dieu.

Now I know how at that fateful moment
those women act
to whom the angel has announced nothing.

They first shriek with delight,
then they sob
and mercilessly dig their nails
into man's flesh.
And as they close their womb
and tauten their muscles
a heart in tumult hurls wild words
up to their lips.

I was beginning to get ready for life
and headed wherever
the world was thickest.
On fairground stalls I well recall the rattle
of rosaries
like rain on a tin roof,

and the girls, as they strolled among the stalls,
nervously clutching their scarves,
liberally cast their sparkling eyes
in all directions,
and their lips launched on the empty air
the delight of kisses to come.

Life is a hard and agonizing flight
of migratory birds
to regions where each man is alone.
And whence there's no return.
And all that you have left behind,
the pain, the sorrows, all your disappointments
seem easier to bear
than is this loneliness,
where there is no consolation
to bring a little comfort to
your tear-stained soul.

What use to me are those sweet sultanas?
Good thing that at the rifle booth I won
a bright-red paper rose!
I kept it a long time
and still it smelled of carbide.

THE CANAL GARDEN

Not till old age did I learn
to love silence.
Sometimes it is more exciting than music.
In the silence emerge tremulous signals
and at the crossroads of memory
you hear names
which time had tried to stifle.

At nightfall in the trees I often hear
even the hearts of birds.
And once in the churchyard
I caught the sound, deep down in a grave,
of a coffin splitting.

On a forgotten stone block in the garden,
hewn in a sea-shell's shape,
the children used to play till dusk.
I can remember it from childhood.
And I'd still see them there.

It probably was the last stone surviving
from an old garden.
Nothing else was left.
Only a fountain and a tree,
only a violated fountain
and a half-shrivelled tree
whose trunk was perforated
by a revolver bullet.

Night, that merciless keeper of darkness,
hurriedly pours the red dawn from the sky
like the bloody water
in which Monsieur Marat was murdered
by a fair-haired beauty's dagger,
and now it begins to rip off people's
own shadows
as a tailor rips off the tacked sleeves
when fitting a jacket.

Everything on earth has happened before,
nothing is new,
but woe to the lovers
who fail to discover a fresh blossom
in every future kiss.

The light still lies on the flower beds
and on the gentle path.
Among the flowers taking a walk
is Count Joseph Emanuel Canal de Malabaile
and with the hem of his exalted cloak
he bends the flower heads
which straighten up again at once.

Jews not admitted!
Well, really!

Each of us walks towards his own abyss.
There are two:
the deep sky overhead and the grave.
The grave is deeper.

By the pool's edge stands the statue of a goddess
hewn from white stone.
The damp sleek curves of her quivering body
are like whipped cream.

Where have your ancient skies gone
where you would tie your flaxen hair
in a honey-hued knot?
With slender arm you cover your breasts
and bend gently forward
as if about to step into the water
which is locked up by pale-pink water lilies
just unfolding.

Your belly, mirrored in the surface,
resembles Orpheus's divine instrument
which the Thracian women wrested from his hands
and flung into the Hebrus.

75

Upon the lintels of the doors they wrote
the year one thousand eight hundred and twenty nine
with hallowed chalk.
In the stalls of the Stavovské Theatre
stood a poet
nervously waiting
for one of the boxes to open
and for the countess to enter.
Deep inside him at that moment screamed
enamoured folly.

He lived in Michalskà Street
at the Red Cockerel,
and since he had no furniture
he wrote his poems lying on the floor,
dipping his pen in an inkstand
pinned to the floorboards.

Be quiet, clumps of roses,
don't whisper her name to me.
Reeds on the lake, be still
and do not rustle,
let me not hear the silk of her skirts
as she leaves for the waiting coach.

Never, never will she stroke
the thin beard on my chin,
never shall I sink my lips
into her body.
I wish I had never seen her,
then she would not have
chopped off my head each time
with the sword of her beauty.

The following day again he stood patiently
by the column in the theatre
fixedly staring at the empty box.
As she came in
she sat down in the velvet armchair

she briefly shut her bewitching eyes
with their long lashes
as a carnivorous plant closes its sticky blooms
from which there's no escape.

Oh shade your eyes, my love,
or I'll go mad.
He was young,
he went mad and died.

Night, eternal ant-heap of the stars,
and what else?
In the green shade of the arbour
the lovers were kissing.

Lips kissed a hundred times
whispering ardent words to
lips kissed a hundred times,
lighting blood's path
pounding to passion's farthest regions.

A pair of daggers,
tongues mutually stabbed
desire-stirred mouths.

The evening star that night was Venus.

Let us return to the noble count.
He was fond of music
and instructed his musicians
to play their wind instruments
concealed in the garden's shrubberies.

The musicians breathed into their instruments
the heavy scent of flowers
and under the touch of their fingers
it changed into love songs
for dancing.

Here they are! If you feel like dancing
dance!

If the coral point
of one of the two rounded hills
of graceful obstinacy
wrote on my coat, as we were dancing,
a few letters from the Morse alphabet
this did not necessarily mean anything.
That happens.
It may even happen by chance.

But I would usually see it as
a call from another planet
orbiting round my forehead.
Someone perhaps will shrug:
What of it?
But I have given all my life
to just this call.

After the dance the weary lady would
sit down on the silky lawn,
spreading the muslin of her ample skirts
around herself
like spreading circles on the water.

I heard her carefree laughter
but I came too late.

As one grows old
one always comes too late,
and in the end one even envies the lawn
two dimples
made by a girl's knees.

I was lucky. Hand in hand
the exhilarated couples danced
on the trampled grass around the trees.
Only once in my life
did I meet that girl.

With a smile she invited me to her side,
the way people invite each other
when they sometimes feel
that a word would be too bold.
Presently she slowed her pace
to let me catch up with her.

Wherever you wish me to follow
I'll gladly go.
Even to the rock where sulphur flowers bloom
close to the crater's rim.

That far she didn't want to go with me.
A shiver ran over her
as if death had touched her.

At least give me your hand — goodbye.
She hesitated briefly
but, for goodbye,
she dug her lips into my mouth
like tiger's claws.

I look at your forehead
as a pilot at his cockpit panel
when he has flown into a storm.
I met you so late
and so unexpectedly.

I know you were hidden
in the deep drift of hair.
It glowed in the dark
but I sought you in vain.

On my empty palm
there was gold dust.

Then you escaped through the fence of your lashes
into your laughter.
And June, in festive garb,
pushed jasmine into our windows.

But in the end you vanished
into the snow of your silence.
How could I even catch a glimpse of you
that far away?
It was cold and dusk began to fall.

You may tear up my poems
and cast the shreds to the wind.
Crumple my letters
and burn them on the fire.

But what will you do with my face
cast in misted metal
no bigger than a hand?
You always had it before your eyes!
Do with it what your disappointment
leads you to do.

But one more time, one last time,
you will hold my head
between your hands.

The count is dead, the countess is dead,
the poet is dead.
The musicians are dead.
All my loves are dead,
and I myself am getting ready
to go.
At least that is how it sometimes seems to me
when I gaze
into your distant eyes
and in the distance vainly seek
the very last stone from the garden
which too is dead.

THE PLAGUE COLUMN
(Excerpts)

To the four corners of the earth they turn:
the four demobilized knights of the heavenly host.
And the four corners of the earth
are barred
behind four heavy locks.

Down the sunny path the ancient shadow
of the Column staggers
from the hour of Shackles
to the hour of Dance.
From the hour of Love
to the hour of the Dragon's Claw.
From the hour of Smiles
to the hour of Wrath.

From the hour of Hope
to the hour of Never,
whence it is just a short step
to the hour of Despair,
to Death's turnstile.

Our lives run
like fingers over sandpaper,
days, weeks, years, centuries.
And there were times when we spent
long years in tears.

I still walk round the Column
where so often I waited,
listening to the water gurgling
from apocalyptic mouths,
always astonished
at the water's flirtatiousness
as it splintered on the basin's surface
until the Column's shadow fell across your face.

That was the hour of the Rose.

You there, young lad, do me a favour: climb
up on the fountain and read out to me
the words the four Evangelists are writing
on their stone pages.

The Evangelist Matthew is first.
        And which of us from pure joy
        can add to his life's span
        one cubit?

And what does Mark, the second, write?
        Is a candle brought
        to be put under a bushel
        and not to be set on a candlestick?

And the Evangelist Luke?
        The light of the body is the eye.
        But where many bodies are
        thither will many eagles be gathered
        together.

And lastly John, the favourite of the Lord,
what does he write?
He has his book shut on his lap.
Then open it, boy. If needs be
with your teeth.

I was christened on the edge of Olšany
in the plague chapel of Saint Roch.

When bubonic plague was raging in Prague
they laid the dead around the chapel.
Body upon body in layers.
Their bones, over the years, grew into
rough-stacked pyres
which blazed
in the quicklime whirlwind of clay.

For a long time I would visit
these mournful places
but I did not forsake the sweetness of life.

I felt happy in the warmth of human breath
and when I roamed among people
I tried to catch the perfume of women's hair.

On the steps of the Olšany taverns
I used to crouch at night to hear
the coffin-bearers and grave-diggers
singing their rowdy songs.

But that was long ago,
the taverns have fallen silent,
the grave-diggers in the end
buried each other.

When spring came within reach
with feather and lute
I'd walk around the lawn with the Japanese cherries
on the south side of the chapel
and, bewitched by their spring splendour,
I thought about girls
silently undressing at night.
I did not know their names
but one of them,
when sleep would not come,
tapped softly on my window.

And who was it that wrote
those poems on my pillow?

Sometimes I would stand by the wooden belfry.
The bell was tolled
whenever they lifted up a corpse in the chapel.
It too is silent now.

I gazed on the classicist statuary
in the Little City cemetery.
The statues were still grieving over their dead
from whom they'd had to part.
Leaving, they walked slowly
with the smile of their ancient beauty.

And there were among them not only women
but also soldiers with helmets, and armed
unless I'm mistaken.

I haven't been here for a long time.

Don't let them dupe you
that the plague's at an end:
I've seen too many coffins hauled
through this dark gateway
which isn't the only one.

The plague still rages and it seems the doctors
are giving different names to the disease
to avoid a panic.
Yet it is still the same old death
and nothing else,
and it is so contagious
no one alive can escape it.

Whenever I have looked out of my window
emaciated horses have been drawing that ill-boding cart
with a shrivelled coffin.
Only those bells aren't tolled so often now,
crosses no longer painted on front doors,
juniper twigs no longer burnt for fumigation.

In the Julian Fields
we'd sometimes lie at nightfall,
when Brno was sinking into darkness,
and on the backwater of the Svitava
the frogs began their plaint.

84

Once a young gipsy sat down beside us.
Her blouse was half unbuttoned
and she read our hands.
To Halas she said:
                    You won't live to be fifty.
To Arthur Černík:
                    You'll live until just after that.
I didn't want her to tell my fortune,
I was afraid.

She seized my hand
and angrily exclaimed:
                    You'll live a long time!
It sounded like a threat.

The many rondels and the songs I wrote!
There was a war all over the world
and all over the world
was grief.
And yet I whispered into bejewelled ears
verses of love.
It makes me feel ashamed.
But no, not really.

A wreath of sonnets I laid upon
the curves of your lap as you fell asleep.
It was more beautiful than the laurel wreaths
of speedway winners.

But suddenly we met
at the steps of the fountain,
we each went somewhere else, at another time
and by another path.

For a long time I felt
I was meeting your feet,
sometimes I even heard your laughter
but it wasn't you.
And finally I even saw your eyes.
But only once.

The worst is over now,
I tell myself: I'm old.
The worst is yet to come:
I'm still alive.
If you really must know:
I have been happy.
Sometimes a whole day, sometimes whole hours,
sometimes just a few minutes.

All my life I have been faithful to love.
And if a woman's hands are more than wings
what then are her legs?
How I enjoyed testing their strength.
That soft strength in their grip.
Let then those knees crush my head!

If I closed my eyes in this embrace
I would not be so drunk
and there wouldn't be that feverish drumming
in my temples.
But why should I close them?

With open eyes
I have walked through this country.
It's beautiful — but you know that.
It has meant more to me perhaps than all my loves
and her embrace has lasted all my life.
When I was hungry
I fed almost daily
on the words of her songs.

Those who have left,
hastily fled to distant lands
must realize it by now:
the world is terrible.
They do not love and are not loved.
We at least love.

So let her knees then crush
my head!

* * *

What's all this talk of grey hair
and wisdom?
When the bush of life burns down
experience is worthless.
Indeed it always is.

After the hailstorm of graves
the Column was thrust up high
and four old poets
leaned on it with their backs
to write on the books' pages
their bestsellers.

The basin now is empty,
littered with cigarette stubs
and the sun only hesitantly uncovers
the grief of the stones pushed aside.
A place perhaps for begging.

But to cast my life away just like that
for nothing at all — that
I won't do.

MERRY-GO-ROUND WITH WHITE SWAN

Where the pavement had turned into tufts of grass
and the electric wires into swallows' wings
two carbide lamps
were lit every evening in spring
and swiftly engulfed by the night,
and the ancient merry-go-round started turning.

The pool of light was quietly avoided
by the late couples
who hugged each other under the thick shrub of darkness
dotted with stars.

For the most beautiful of all gods
is Love.
It always has been thus, and everywhere,
not only in distant turquoise Greece
but even in our lousy Žižkov quarter,
where the city either began
or ended. Whichever you like.
And where the singing in the taverns
went on till dawn.

On the edge among the horses' hooves
grandly and elegantly an aristocratic swan
sailed past,
as if snatched straight from a poem by Mallarmé.
And spread its wings.

That afternoon there was a brief shower
that made even the trampled grass smell sweet,
and the evening, full of vernal yearnings,
slowly melted into night.

The hurdy-gurdy had just begun
to chop up a new tune
when a girl with a silver bracelet
stepped into the swan's wings.

I noticed her wrist
because she embraced the swan's neck
and her eyes
looked past my enflamed glances.

In the end she looked at me
and smiled a little,
and next time round she waved to me,
the third time round blew me a kiss.
That was all.

I waited for her next appearance,
ready to jump on board and join her,
but the swan's wings were empty.

Love sometimes is like the flower
of the wild poppy:
you can't carry it home.
But the two lamps were hissing loud
like a pair of snakes,
snake confronting snake,
and I was vainly chasing after her feet
into the vast darkness.

There was a time when they fired a cannon on the walls
to announce midday,
and for a breath-long second the hustle stopped.
Some women are Morning, some are Noontide
and some are Evening.

Hesitant fingers gently roaming
over the skin of shyness,
until modesty and fear begin to flee from the places
we so love,
and a wave of nakedness, wave after wave,
floods our mouths and eyes and cheeks
and again returns to our lips
as to the shore.

Thus our blood began to flow
into our veins
and thence to the heart and from the heart
back into our arteries.

Neither greed for power nor thirst for glory
are as dizzy
as the passions of love.
Even if perhaps
I wasn't one of those
to be granted overmuch
I gratefully kissed its feet.

When it appears to me that women today
are maybe more beautiful
than they were in my youth
this is only delusion and surmise.
Nothing but bitter nostalgia. And regrets.

Not long ago I was looking at
the yellowed photographs of Mucha's models
in his Paris studio.
The startling charm of these long bygone women
took my breath away.

There were two wars, disease and famine
and a cluster of suffering.
Life was not good on earth in those days.
But it was truly our life
no matter how it was.

I used to yearn for distant cities
in colourful strange countries
even on the edge of the desert.
Now they are rapidly receding
like the stars in the age-old darkness.
There is a chill in the cathedrals
and women's smiles
have become rare and strange and faraway
like blooms in the jungle.

Only the yearning has remained: not to be so lonely,
and my curiosity.
And daily I am catechized by these.
I am thankful our women do not wear
a veil down to their ankles.
But inexorable time now presses me
and forcibly leads me elsewhere.

Goodbye. In all my life I never committed
any betrayal.
That I am aware of
and you may believe me.

But the most beautiful of all gods
is Love.

A CHAPLET OF SAGE
(For František Hrubín)

Noon was approaching and the quiet
was cut by the buzzing of the flies
as though with a diamond.
We were lying in the grass by the Sázava,
drinking Chablis
chilled in a forest spring.

Once at Konopiště Castle
I was allowed to view
an ancient dagger from a display case.
Only in the wound did a secret spring
release a triple blade.
Poems are sometimes like that.
Not many of them perhaps,
but it is difficult to extract them from the wound.

A poet often is like a lover.
He easily forgets
his one-time whispered promise of gentleness
and the most fragile gracefulness
he treats with brutal gesture.

He has the right to rape.
Under the banner of beauty
or that of pain.
Or under the banner of both.
Indeed it is his mission.

Events themselves hand him
a ready pen
that with its tip he may indelibly tattoo
his message.

Not on the skin of the breast
but straight into the muscle
which throbs with blood.
But rose and heart are not just love,
nor a ship a voyage or adventure,
nor a knife murder,
nor an anchor fidelity unto death.

These foolish symbols lie.
Life has long outgrown them.
Reality is totally different
and a lot worse still.

And so the poet drunk with life
should spew out all bitterness,
anger and despair,
rather than let his song become a tinkling bell
on a sheep's neck.

When we had drunk our fill
and rose from the flattened grass
a bunch of naked children on the bank
hopped into the river below us.
And one of the young girls,
the one who on her straw-blonde hair
wore a chaplet of wet sage,
climbed up on a large rock
to stretch out on the sun-warmed stone.

We had a slight shock:
                    Good Lord,
she's no longer a child!

THE SMOKE OF MARIJUANA

To bow at the footlight
and sink into a curtsey,
as the French do on the stage —

no, that's not for me.
But no sooner had I written
a few happy lines about love
than my eyes would seek the eyes of women,
my hands their hands
and my lips their startled lips.

God knows, in this country
women like poetry.
Maybe that's why the poet's sighs
don't make them press their hands so frantically
upon their breasts.

When I was still young
and learned to woo women,
oh, my conceit
was more pretentious
than a peacock's fan,
which is blue and pink and golden
like Renoir's palette.

Deceiving myself thus
I happily came to the end,
to despair, which some call wisdom.
I can't think why.

But at that moment someone at my back
whispered into my ear:
Like marijuana smoke
are poet's verses.

And if that perfumed smoke
opens the door to some exotic country,
whence delicious moments of happiness, smiling,
run up to meet us,
holding hands
with happy moments of delight —
why shouldn't poetry achieve it too?

One single song is enough
to make people catch their breath
and make girls, when they hear it,
burst into tears.

AND NOW GOODBYE

To all those million verses in the world
I've added just a few.
They probably were no wiser than a cricket's chirrup.
I know. Forgive me.
I'm coming to the end.

They weren't even the first footmarks
in the lunar dust.
If at times they sparkled after all
it was not their light.
I loved this language.

And that which forces silent lips
to quiver
will make young lovers kiss
as they stroll through red-gilded fields
under a sunset
slower than in the tropics.

Poetry is with us from the start.
Like loving,
like hunger, like the plague, like war.
At times my verses were embarrassingly foolish.

But I make no excuse.
I believe that seeking beautiful words
is better
than killing and murdering.

AUTOBIOGRAPHY

Sometimes,
when she would talk about herself,
my mother said:
My life was sad and quiet,
I always walked on tip-toe.
But if I got a little angry
and stamped my foot
the cups, which had been my mother's,
would tinkle on the dresser
and make me laugh.

At the moment of my birth, so I am told,
a butterfly flew in by the window
and settled on my mother's bed,
but that same moment a dog howled in the yard.
My mother thought it
a bad omen.

My life of course has not been quite
as peaceful as hers.
But even though I gaze upon our present days
with wistfulness
as if at empty picture frames
and all I see is a dusty wall,
still it has been so beautiful.

There are many moments
I cannot forget,
moments like radiant flowers
in all possible colours and hues,
while evenings filled with fragrance
resembled purple grapes
hidden in the leaves of darkness.

With passion I read poetry
and loved music
and blundered, ever surprised,
from beauty to beauty.
But when I first saw
the picture of a nude woman
I began to believe in miracles.

My life unrolled swiftly.
It was too short
for my vast longings
which had no bounds.
Before I knew it
my life's end was drawing near.

Death soon will kick open my door
and enter.
With startled terror at that minute
I'll catch my breath
and forget to breathe again.

May I not be denied the time
once more to kiss the hands
of her who patiently and with my steps
walked on and on and on
and who loved most of all.

THE HUNT FOR THE KINGFISHER

How many times has not a verse come to my mind
even at the crossroads
while the lights were at red!
Why not?
You can even fall in love
in that short time.

But before I'd crossed over
to the far side
I'd forgotten the verses.
Then I was still able
to jot them down off-hand.
But the smile
of the girl who crossed over in front of me
I remember to this day.

Under the railway bridge at Kralupy
I often as a boy would climb
into the branches of a hollow willow
and among the twigs above the river
would think and dream
of my first verses.

But, to be honest, I also
would think and dream
of lovemaking and women
and watch the torn-off reeds
float on the water.

Easter was around the corner,
the air was full of vernal magic.
I even saw a kingfisher once
on a whipping twig.

In all my life
I never saw another
and yet my eyes have often longed
to see that delicate beauty closer.

Even the river had a pungent fragrance then,
that bitter-sweet fragrance,
the fragrance of women's loosened hair
when from their shoulders it overflows
their naked bodies.

And when, years later, I immersed
my face into that hair
and opened my eyes,
I gazed through those sunlit depths
to the roots of love.

There are rare moments in my life
when I find myself once more
under the railway bridge at Kralupy.
Everything there is as it used to be,
even that willow —
but I am just imagining it all.

Easter is once more round the corner,
the air is full of vernal magic
and the river is fragrant.

For every day under my window
the birds go mad quite early in the morning
and, singing as if their lives depended on it,
they drown each other's voices,
and those sweet dreams
which usually come at dawn
are gone.

But that's the only thing
I can reproach spring for.

FINGER PRINTS

Even by force I make the night surrender
pleasant dreams.
Alas, mostly in vain.
But life, at least, allows us
to return against the current of time
not without vertigo, but with some slight regret
and a tear of sadness,
all the way
to where our memory reaches.

Remembrances, however, have a woman's skin.
When you taste them with the tip of your tongue
they taste sweet
and have an exciting fragrance.
So what!

The statue of the Vltava river by Václav Pachner
in the façade of the Clam-Gallas palace
pours from its jug
a stream of water
intertwined with stars.
She has long bewitched my eyes
with her shapely nudity.

Confused they strayed a long time
over her body,
not knowing where to settle first.
On her delightful face
or on the virgin charms
of her lily-of-the-valley breasts
which so often are the crown
of all the beauty of the female form
in all parts of the world.

I must have been fourteen,
or maybe a year older,
as I stood bewildered,
as if waiting
for her to raise her eyes to me
and smile.

One moment when I thought
no one was watching
I managed, from the basin's edge,
to clasp her leg in my palm.
Higher I didn't get.
It was rough, it was made of sandstone,
and it was cold.
It was still snowing lightly.
But a hot wave of desire
like an electric shock
surged through my blood.

But if love is something more
than a mere touch,
and it is that,
a drop of dew can sometimes be enough,
suddenly trickling down on to your hand
from a flower petal.
Your head suddenly spins
as if your thirsty lips had gulped
some heavy wine.

In the doorway of the Clementinum nearby
stood a policeman.
And while the wind was ruffling
the cock's tail feather on his hat
he looked around.

He could have easily run me in.
No doubt I'd left my finger prints
on the girl's calf.
Perhaps I had committed an offence
against public morality,
I don't know!
I know nothing about the law.
Yet I was sentenced after all
to lifelong punishment.

If love is a labyrinth
full of glittering mirrors,
and it is that,
I'd crossed its threshold
and entered.

And from the bewitching glitter of mirrors
I haven't found the way out
to this day.

NOVEMBER RAIN

How defenceless a sleeper is at night!
When cruel and senseless dreams
attack him
he calls for help in his sleep.
And yet these are just worthless coins
in a pocket with holes in.

I do not like those nocturnal incidents
when darkness begins to relate
yesterday's adventures.
Dreams hurtle from darkness into shadows,
they can't stand daylight.
No hand controls their reins,
the halter-bells don't dance.
They're mute.

Those dreams with half-closed eyes
are happier.
I can summon up whomsoever I wish,
even those who left us long ago
and whom I loved.
They willingly come to me
and prolong their lives
by those few moments.

It was raining, it was November.
I was sitting in the train, on my way to the cemetery
to visit my dead.
The drops were spattering against the window
and the glass was like a ruffled mirror.
And smiling at me, from its surface, was
a girl's face.

— Why, I have almost forgotten you
and you still smile at me?

— I've long ceased to be jealous of anyone
and I have long disdained all hope.
You see me as a young girl, just like then,
I'm dead but I'm not getting any older.

I no longer exist, and I am nothing,
all I can give you is a sweet memory.
It may inflame you like a sip of wine
but won't intoxicate.
And no hangover either.

— Do you still remember?
I used to read poetry late into the night.
Sometimes the crowing of the cock
sent me to bed.

— And I have dropped all shame:
I come to meet you of my own intent
and I myself unbutton my bodice.
Embrace me.
Even the dead have need of a little love
when they've so far to walk
to the very end of eternity.

— If you still think of me sometime
write me a few verses.
I'm curious.

The train was pulling into the station
and the girl's face was lost to me
among the drops on the window.
As I was leaving the station concourse
I didn't look where I was going
and people bumped into me.
But two days later I was whispering these verses
into the dead locks on her temple.

BERTHE SOUCARET

When Berthe Soucaret,
an unknown Creole girl from Guadeloupe,
was eighteen
she was elected beauty queen.

She was the first queen in the world
and all women
at once looked at their mirrors.

That was at Spa in Belgium,
that town of bubbles, flowers and of song,
on 18th September 1888.
On a dust-covered music box,
dug up among some junk in the attic,
I found the same year marked
in golden figures.
The music box played one of the love songs
of Franz Schubert.

A lot of years had passed
since her coronation
and she had long been dead
when I fell in love
with her shadow
I had encountered in my youth.
From that moment I have sought that beauty
in the features of those
towards whom I was running.

Why cannot every woman —
at least some time, at least for a while,
at least for one pair of eyes —
be the most beautiful woman in the world?

Fingers straying over the body's firmament
like stars over the sky,
until her whole body flares up
with the flame burning within.
Lips drinking from lips
and thirst is not assuaged
and longing for delight leads both of them
to the ancient ritual.

What more beautiful gift has life to give
than love?
Garlanded with the green boughs
of its earthiness
it is nearest to heaven
and it alone offers a glimpse
of how happy we should probably be
if only —

Soon the woman brushes all the kisses
from her burning face
and with both hands
reaches up to her loosened hair
to hold back for a short while
the fugitive gleam of her crown.

One girl will come, and then another
after many years.
In the flowered dress of memories
she will rustle with words so soft
I can hardly hear them.
But presently they disappear again,
one after another,
and I must bury them again
in the nocturnal darkness,
back to the darkness whence they came
and that is even blacker!
No longer tears, no longer a torch,
and maybe forever.

Among those who came was Berthe Soucaret,
the young Creole girl from the island of Guadeloupe
which smells of vanilla.
Maybe she was the most beautiful of all.
Maybe. I don't remember.

Don't go away just yet
and do believe me:
I had to fall upon my knees
before your beauty then,
and only in my dream I kissed
its feet, even though you were already dead.

Whenever I remember you
to this day
I hear my old heart beating.

As for those memories which were not pleasant
and those which had no love,
I've left them lying by the road,
a prey to condors.

THE MISTRESS OF THE POETS

Those foolish moments of first love!
I still believed then that
to die amidst spring blossom
if you are in love
head over heels,
or to die at the Venice carnival,
can be more beautiful
than in bed at home.

But death is the lady of all pains
known to the world.
Her train is woven
from the rattle in the throat of the dying
and embroidered with the stars of tears.

Death is the lute of lamentations,
the torch of burning blood,
the urn of love
and the door to nowhere.

Sometimes death is the mistress of the poets.
Let them court her
in the stench of dead flowers,
if they can bear
the tolling of the gloomy bells
which are now on the march,
stamping through bloody mud.

Death slips into the female body
with its long narrow hand
and chokes the infants under the heart.
True, they may go to paradise,
but still all bloody.

Death is the empress of all killing
and her sceptre
has from the origin of the world
commanded the horrors of war . . .

Death is the younger sister of decay,
the messenger of ruin and nothingness,
and her hands
push upon everybody's breast
the burden of the grave.

But death is also just an instant,
a scratching of the pen
and no more.

LUNAR IRONMONGERY

Of love, perhaps, or perhaps of women
one might talk at greater length —
but our talks of poetry,
of the beauty of verses,
of the mystery of words,
were likewise endless,
good Lord!

Night would begin to pale,
the impatient dew would fall
sometimes when I accompanied
the poet Hora
along that long Plzeňská Road
to Košíře.

When we passed the Little City cemetery,
where death has now long ceased to live,
the graveyard still resembled a chessboard
set for a game.
Shortly the game would start
between the darkness and the first red dawn.

The Moon, that lovely lady,
was behind our backs that night.
She belonged to the romantic poets
and her beauty
was passed on by the dead to the living
like a gold ring.
She last belonged to Mácha.

Hora has long been dead,
he died young.
When spring comes
and in his garden in Hořín
the fruit trees burst into blossom
to remind us of the tender bloom
and brittleness of his verses

I hurry over to Vyšehrad, to the Hall of Fame.
I have a key.

Inside I knock at the plaque of the niche
with his name.
But there is the silence of the grave.
Only once did I think
I heard a soft sigh.

I still return to the places
he used to love,
and I feel as if I were stroking
an amorous fold of velvet.

I used to sit quite near the tomb
of the Passau Bishop Thun-Hohenstein,
who has been kneeling in the Little City cemetery,
hands folded,
these one hundred and fifty years.

Perhaps I wasn't there alone.
Indeed I wasn't,
when abruptly from the evening sky
a spring shower came down.
We sheltered in the Plague Chapel,
by the cemetery gate:
its door was shut
by the wind alone.

Through the cracked window the moonlight fell
into the chapel,
so palely brilliant, brilliantly pale,
illuminating a frightened face.
The light was cold
like a dead man's hand,
but the girl's lips were hot
and tasted of raindrops.
At that moment there wasn't anything more beautiful
in all the world.

My Lord Bishop, pray
for me too!

The changes that have taken place
in those few years!
The chapel has long been pulled down
and rain no longer falls for me
at intimate moments.
Even the Moon who now tiptoes
into the rectangle of my window
is no longer the same.

The moment when a human foot
first stepped on her
she was already dead.
She'd died a few minutes earlier,
as soon as men with their instruments
began to float down on
her cold nakedness.

What we now see in the sky
is just a dead satellite,
and the jaws of its craters
chew upon nothingness.

Her ripped-off rose-red veils
she drags across the sky
and treads on them in the heavenly mud.

She continues orbiting the Earth,
but without any real meaning now,
as at the creation of the world,
complete with all that ironmongery
left behind
by the happy Americans.

AN UMBRELLA FROM PICCADILLY

If you're at your wits' end with love
try falling in love again —
say, with the Queen of England.
Why not?
Her features are on every postage stamp
of that ancient kingdom.
But if you were to ask her
for a date in Hyde Park
you can bet on it
you'd wait in vain.

If you've any sense at all
you'll wisely tell yourself:
Why of course, I know:
it's raining in Hyde Park today.

When he was coming back from England
my son bought me in London's Piccadilly
an elegant umbrella.
Whenever necessary
I now have above my head
my own small sky
which may be black
but in its tensioned wire spokes
God's mercy may be flowing like
electric current.

I open my umbrella even when it's not raining,
as a canopy
over the volume of Shakespeare's sonnets
I carry with me in my pocket.

But there are moments when I am frightened
even by the sparkling bouquet of the universe.
Outstripping its beauty
it threatens us with its infinity
and that is all too similar
to the sleep of death.

It also threatens us with the void and frostiness
of its thousands of stars
which at night delude us
with their gleam.

The one we have named Venus
is downright terrifying.
Its rocks are still on the boil
and like gigantic waves of the sea
mountains are rising up
and burning sulphur falls.

We always ask where hell is.
It is there!

But what use is a fragile umbrella
against the universe?
Besides I don't even carry it.
I have enough of a job
to walk along,
clinging close to the ground
as a nocturnal moth in daytime
to the coarse bark of a tree.

All my life I have sought the paradise
that used to be here,
whose traces I have found
only on women's lips
and in the curves of their skin
when it was warm with love.

All my life I've longed
for freedom.
At last I've discovered the door
that leads to it.
It is death.

Now that I'm old
some charming woman's face
will sometimes waft between my lashes
and her smile will stir my blood.

Shyly I turn my head
and remember the Queen of England
whose features are on every postage stamp
of that ancient kingdom.
God save the Queen!

Oh yes, I know quite well:
it's raining in Hyde Park today.

LOST PARADISE

The Old Jewish Cemetery
is one great bouquet of grey stone
on which time has trodden.
I was drifting among the graves,
thinking of my mother.
She used to read the Bible.

The letters in two columns
welled up before her eyes
like blood from a wound.
The lamp was guttering and smoking
and Mother put on her glasses.
At times she had to blow it out
and with her hairpin straighten
the glowing wick.

But when she closed her tired eyes
she dreamed of Paradise,
before God had garrisoned it
with armed cherubim . . .
Often she fell asleep over the Book
which slipped from her lap.

I was still young
when I discovered in the Old Testament
those fascinating verses about love
and eagerly searched for
the passages on incest . . .
That time I did not yet suspect
how much tenderness is hidden in the names
of Old Testament women.

Adah is Ornament and Orpah
is a Hind,
Naamah is the Pleasant
and Nikol is the Little Brook.
Abigail is the Fount of Exultation.

But if I recall how helplessly I watched
as they dragged off the Jews,
even the crying children,
I still shudder with horror
and a chill runs down my spine.

Jemima is the Dove and Tamar
a Palm Tree.
Tirzah is Pleasantness
and Zilpah a Raindrop.
My God, how beautiful this is.

We were living in hell
yet no one dared to strike the weapon
from the murderers' hands.
As if within our hearts we did not have
a spark of humanity!

The name Jecholiah means
The Lord is Mighty.
And yet their frowning God
gazed over the barbed wire
and did not move a finger —

Delilah is the Delicate, Rachel
the Ewe Lamb,
Deborah the Bee
and Esther the Bright Star.

I'd just returned from the cemetery
when the June evening with its scents
leaned against the windows.
But from the silent distance now and then came thunder
of a future war.
There is no time without murder.

I almost forgot:
Rhoda is the Rose.
And this flower perhaps is the only thing
that's left us on earth
from ancient Paradise.

THE ROYAL PAVILION

The times I've searched through southern pine groves
under the sun of Tuscany
and wandered along ruined walls
and scattered dried-up wells
over whose crumbling sides
ivy was creeping.

The times I've sat gazing,
on the benches of ancient cathedrals
and before altars, at those famous women
whose heads were garlanded
with the verses of poets
and whose beauty sat like a jewel
on the breast of Italy.

Today I am too old —
but neither in memories nor in dreams
do legs get tired.

Last night there was a full moon.
In the Chotek Gardens
it was as light as day
and lovers were trying in vain
to conceal their kisses.

On the white foreheads of the marble statues
by the small grotto
the moonlight fell that night,
and the faces, normally so gentle,
were frightening
like the faces of the dead
rising from their graves.

The fountain fell silent, the water was slumbering
and the delicate bellies of a thousand droplets
ceased to beat against the wet metal.

Only the small fieldmice
under the fountain
were scurrying about the garden flowers
as in a maze.

To this day someone is raising the torch
which tints the roofs green
to light the path, when the dance is ended,
for the girl dancers' weary feet —
just a few steps.

When they had all gone
the columns in the empty arcades moved off
and like mute pilgrims
set out on their pilgrimage.
They walked without heads
and without legs and without arms
and without rosaries
with only their broken shadows
all about the pavilion.

At that moment the curtains across the sky
abruptly parted
and before my eyes appeared the Cathedral
and below it the Castle
with all the towers of the ancient battlements.

Whenever I gaze out on Prague
— and I do so constantly and always with bated breath
because I love her —
I turn my mind to God
wherever he may hide from me,
beyond the starry mists
or just behind that moth-eaten screen,
to thank him
for granting me that magnificent setting to live in.
To me and to my joys and carefree loves,
to me and to my tears without weeping
when the loves departed,

and to my more-than-bitter grief
when even my verses could not weep.
I love her fire-charred walls
to which we clung during the war
so as to hold out.
I would not change them for anything in the world.
Not even for others,
not even if the Eiffel Tower rose between them
and the Seine flowed sadly past,
not even for all the gardens of paradise
full of flowers.

When I shall die — and this will be quite soon —
I shall still worry in my heart
about this city's destiny.

And mercilessly, just as Marsyas,
let anyone be flayed alive
who lays hands on this city,
no matter who he is.
No matter how sweetly he plays
on his flute.

TO BE A POET

Life taught me long ago
that music and poetry
are the most beautiful things on earth
that life can give us.
Except for love, of course.

In an old textbook,
published by the Imperial Printing House
in the year of Vrchlický's death,
I looked up the section on poetics
and poetic ornament.

Then I placed a rose in a tumbler,
lit a candle
and started to write my first verses.

Flare up, then, flame of words,
and soar,
even if my fingers get burned!

A startling metaphor is worth more
than a ring on one's finger.
But not even Puchmajer's Rhyming Dictionary
was any use to me.

In vain I snatched for ideas
and frantically closed my eyes
in order to hear that first magic line.
But in the dark, instead of words,
I saw a woman's smile and
wind-blown hair.

That's been my destiny.
Behind it I've been staggering breathlessly
all through my life.

THE BOMBING OF THE TOWN OF KRALUPY

KRALUPY IS NOT A BEAUTIFUL TOWN ...

Kralupy is not a beautiful town
and never was.
On its edge smokestacks have sprung up
like phantom trees without branches,
without leaves, without blossoms, without bees
and without birds.

As you got off the train,
still on the carriage step
you'd breathe the sweetish stench
of the Maggi factory.
It stood quite near the station.

But I would waste no time and hasten
to a quiet door,
where several pairs of open arms awaited me
into which I happily fell.

To this day — how many years have passed? —
when I close my eyes
and look into the semidarkness of my lids
I see the smiling faces
of those I loved.
But they are pale now
like stars on a winter afternoon
when dusk is just gathering.

Towards nightfall and especially before rain
people would shut their windows.
Flakes of soot descended on the town
and a mist filled the streets
like autumnal fog
but armed to the teeth.

Yet to this day they're blooming there for me
even on the barbed wire —
those briars.
You need only to stop a while
and draw a quiet breath.

THE CANDLESTICK

God knows what happened to the candlestick
my mother brought with her from Kralupy.
It was made from an artillery shell-case
of the First World War
and for many years it stood on top of our cupboard.

Whenever we ran out of paraffin at home
we put a candle in the candlestick:
it burnt with a sooty flame.

By its poor light
I wrote my first verses.
And when my folk went to bed
I read, while it was burning,
novels about love.

Its trembling flame
became my inescapable will-o'-the-wisp
which lured me from my lessons,
at least in my dreams,
into Prague's mildewy little streets,
where love was quick and short.

But I was afraid.
                  They were more mysterious
than the treacherous swamps of the Jizera
near its headwaters,
where even a bold horseman drowned
with his horse.

Whenever my mother buffed up the candlestick
with a velvet pad
she seemed to me to draw a deep sigh.
I did not ask her why.
Later I guessed the reason.
Let there be no more war.

But it came!

THE CASHMERE SHAWL

It's a long time since lilies-of-the-valley
grew in the Kralupy woods,
as they did in my boyhood,
when I fell in love
with my mother's youngest sister.
She was a few years older than me
and she was beautiful.
Everyone said so.

I knew so little about women then,
and yet my thoughts ceaselessly
revolved round womanhood.
She'd move around me
with just a quiet smile
but never looked me in the eyes
which were burning
as my blood silently exploded
in my veins.

The times I flung my arms wide open
to embrace at least the air
through which she had just passed,
carrying her sweet smile with her
to the next room.

Often I daringly longed
to see her naked,
at least in my dreams.
Or at least naked to her waist,
so that my lips, still innocent of such things,
might bend down close
to her rosy shadows.

When sometimes she had hurried off somewhere,
leaving her cashmere shawl
flung over a chair-back,
I'd press it to my face
and inhale its fragrance.

My vacation was over and I was leaving
for Prague again.
In parting she gave me her hand
and I took it carefully in mine
as if it were a delicate orchid bloom.

It's a long time since lilies-of-the-valley
grew in the Kralupy woods.
It's a long time!

THE KRALUPY CORSO

The Zakolany stream in the town
was an obstacle and smelled.
Heaven could no longer bear to watch it.
It carried with it all kinds of effluent
and those who lived nearby
would chuck their broken crockery into it
and their dead cats.

Paplhám, the hideous down-and-out,
with whom parents scared their children,
collected from the city's refuse dumps
old rags,
soaked with sweat, with tears and blood.
People were glad to get rid of them,
often to wipe out memories.
And in the stream the beggar washed his feet.

When they built the bridge in Kralupy
they paved the stream over.

But from the day
the water fell silent between the stones
the birds stopped singing
in the trees along the stream.

From the church right across the square,
past Nývlt's bookshop
— I still can see his shopwindow before me
and in the glass my face —
and on down to the stream:
this used to be the Kralupy corso.

That was also the route taken by the priest
in his white vestments under a blue sky,
on Corpus Christi day,
and his specially polished boots
mercilessly crushed the flowers
strewn in his path by the young girls.

With a head full of gilded plans
and verses,
which I whispered to myself on the way,
I joined the corso with my timid
steps of yearning.

My friend, the actor Špál,
would stand in the winter on Palacký Bridge
and count the swans on the river.
I've never counted anything in my life,
not swans, not days, not nights,
not even money.
Life nowadays is all figures,
but what was I to count then?
The drops of rain?

Or the strings inside me,
of which the poets write so often?
They had just been touched
                    by the fingers of my first longing.

Or maybe kisses?
Those were then still scant.
Or girls' shy smiles?
Ah yes!
        Smile after smile
till the wind carried them away.

The moment midday would be rung
I'd hurry home
and in the sweat of my brow all afternoon
I'd write poetry.

Only a little way beyond the river
Mr Hálek was born.
When he fell in love
he shook amorous verses
from the sleeves of his frock-coat.

On my love's threshold,
who'd crossed my path,
I laid this message:
— I am well aware
that my verses aren't much good.
As you read them
I'll plead with your eyes
not to be angry with me.
And to my humble poems
I have tied this rose with a silver thread.
If with your lips you touch
its dewy petals
you will be kissing your own beauty.

The day before, when I had cut the rose,
I had to blow
off its rose-red petals —
which opened so amorously
that I was all a-tremble —
an ugly speck of soot.

NIGHT ALARM

The war gave added darkness to our nights
and anxiety to our days.
In every corner hung a sword,
threatened a submachine-gun,
crouched horror.
Revolvers were like lurking rats,
hungry for prey.

I was in Kralupy, waiting for a train.
The war was in its fifth year
and in the silence of the swallows' evening
I was strolling through the town.

Passenger trains ran only after dark
when low-level raiders no longer
threatened from the white clouds.
The town was settling down to sleep.

The clocks had not yet struck ten
when the sirens wailed.
I hastened to hide my fear
under the railway arches.

We used to live not far from here,
in Sokolská Street,
and as a small boy
I experienced a strange encounter
at this very spot.

Reeling from under the arches came
Paplhám, the beggar, with his sack of stinking filth.
He was drunk
and someone flung a stone at him.

The beggar stopped and threatened with his fist
not only his assailant
but the whole town about him
and from the centre of the square
he hurled his beggar's curse:

— May it crash down into its black cellars,
and not the cellars only,
but into even blacker despair,
down to the bottom of its tears!
Let fire, fire, fire
strike from the heights of heaven on this town,
like burning wings of hungry vultures
on a new cadaver
and consummate its ruin!
Amen.

The beggar has long exchanged
his tight-fisted doorsteps
for other kingdoms
but his curse has remained
like a black mark among the clouds
spattered with oily soot.

The All-Clear sounded
a few minutes later
and we left our shelter.
The night was heavy with perfume
and the sky full of stars.

May nights used to belong to lovers,
good Lord!

From Nelahozevsí came the whistle of the train,
it was high time.
I hurried to the platform.
But no sooner had I sat down in the train
than I felt a bitter sense
of fleeing from this town
which I love,
of abandoning it at the moment
of its danger.

But the station building vanished
in the spring darkness
and the train moved on to Dolany,
where all was blossom.

THE BLOW

Our black-out was by then threadbare
and the light shone through.
The days were dripping away slowly,
like honey from a wooden spoon
and faithful but impatient hope
was short of breath.
Time this accursed war came to an end!
High time!

At last the sixth winter had rolled through the land.
The grass swiftly stripped off
its snowy shift
which by now was no longer clean,
and stood naked.

On the day of the equinox,
when astronomical spring begins
I used to go to Kralupy
to visit a deserted grave.

All those I knew at the time
were now long dead,
only the girl in this grave
was still alive.

She'd been the first to breathe into my face
the sharp flame of love,
but at the same time fiercely defended
her matutinal beauty,
and I still lacked the courage
for amorous violence.

She died on the first day of spring,
she was nineteen.
So quiet, meek and gentle
afraid of love.

But she had no fear of death
and died bravely with a smile
in her feverish eyes.

As the sirens sounded
I stood at her grave.
                And now I know
why I came a day late.
I was to be present!

The sexton, Mr Ferdinand Žebro,
called out to those who were a little slow.
Allied aircraft were approaching,
it was nearly noon.
The seconds on my wrist were crackling,
the hour of destiny had come.

Near the cemetery they scored a hit
on one of the full storage tanks
of the petroleum refinery.
The oil went up in a sheet of flame
and smoke veiled the town.

Red-hot pieces of metal
landed among the crosses
and new bombs swiftly followed,
now dropped at random
into the black smoke over the town.

I was going to escape from the cemetery,
but the sexton insisted
I stayed
and took cover behind a low grave.
So I lay down beside the one I loved
and put my head by hers.
And the dead girl gave me her hand.

At last we are lying here together
like lovers
after a passionate embrace,
and worn out by a hundred kisses
we now hold hands.

But from the town in quick succession
came new explosions
like thunderous beats on a kettle-drum
shrouded in black.
And the sky with fiery keys
opened up in the Kralupy streets
one crater after another.

The bombing had been going on for an hour
and still there was no end.

Abruptly the explosions stopped,
the scattered aircraft reformed
and flew off somewhere towards Kladno.
When they wanted to sound the All-Clear
in Kralupy
there was no siren left.

For a while I gazed around
the horizon of death
and slowly got to my feet.
Half dead
I staggered to the half-dead town,
terrified at what I would see.

Only the church with its silent tower
remained standing among the ruins,
                    untouched.
On its floor they were laying out the dead,
Catholics, Protestants and unbelievers,
and the church received them all
under its gentle roof.

I do not know if I may say at last
what crossed my mind
at the sight of the bodies
            — it was a shocking thought.

They lay there on the ground in tidy rows
like so many shot hares laid out
after a successful shoot.

NEVER AGAIN

A hundred houses were in ruins,
nearly a thousand had been damaged
by aerial bombs.
No, I didn't count them myself.
I worked my way through the rubble
and circumnavigated the craters.
They were frightening
like gaping gates to fiery hell.

Speedily they cleared away the debris
but it was three days before
they broke into the little house
in Šverma Street,
the house of Mr Hrnčíř.
The whole family was dead.

Only the rooster, that fighting cock
whom the Apostle Peter did not
greatly love,
alone had saved himself.
Over the bodies of the dead he'd climbed
onto a pile of rubble.

He looked about the scene of the disaster
and spread his wings
to shake the heavy dust
from his golden feathers.

And I repeated softly to myself
what I had found written
in letters of grief and in letters of pain
upon the faces of the Kralupy people.

And into that silence of death
I screamed in a loud voice,
so loud the war should hear it:
Never again, war!

The rooster looked at me
with its black beady eye
and burst into horrible laughter.
He laughed at me
and at my pointless screaming.
Besides, he was a bird
and sided with the planes.
The bastard!

VERSES FROM AN OLD TAPESTRY

Prague!
Who has seen her but once
will at least hear her name
always ring in his heart.
She is herself a song woven into time
and we love her.
So let her ring!

My first happy dreams
glittered above her rooftops
like flying saucers
and vanished God knows where
when I was young.

Once I pressed my face
against the stone of an ancient wall
somewhere below the Castle forecourt
and in my ear, suddenly,
sounded a gloomy booming.
That was the roar of bygone centuries.
But the moist soft soil
of the White Mountain
was whispering gently in my ear.

Go forth, you'll be enchanted.
Sing out, they're waiting.
And don't lie!

I went and did not lie.
And to you, my loves,
only a little.

BACH CONCERTO

I never slept late in the morning,
the early trams would wake me,
and often my own verses.
They pulled me out of bed by my hair,
dragged me to my table,
and as soon as I'd rubbed my eyes
they made me write.

Bound by sweet saliva
to the lips of a unique moment,
I gave no thought
to the salvation of my miserable soul,
and instead of eternal bliss
I longed for a quick instant
of fleeting pleasure.

In vain did the bells try to lift me up:
I clung to the ground with tooth and nail.
It was full of fragrance
and exciting mysteries.
And when I gazed at the sky at night
I did not seek the heavens.
I was more afraid of the black holes
somewhere on the edge of the universe,
they are more terrible still
than hell itself.

But I caught the sound of a harpsichord.
It was a concerto
for oboe, harpsichord and strings
by Johann Sebastian Bach.
From where it came I do not know.
But clearly not from earth.

Although I had not drunk any wine
I swayed a little
and had to steady myself with
my own shadow.

NOCTURNAL DIVERTIMENTO

ALLEGRO NON TANTO

It's getting dark. But don't turn on the light.
I like to look at your eyes
                        in the dusk.
Tell me then! How's Vienna?

Do they still sell in the market
bunches of lavender,
that sweet fragrance of bygone loves
from the end of the millenium?
My mother used to put them in her wardrobe
against the moths.

And do they still dance in Vienna
till the chandeliers shake?

And what about the women?
                Do the pretty Viennese
still put their lips to lips
so willingly and so gently,
only to sink the thorn of love
the more deeply
straight into the heart?

Besides, that happens even here
often enough.
                You don't believe me?
It even happened to me,
what's more, in the night express
from Prague to Berlin.

And what about the men? Do they still not guess
how shamefully they buried
their Amadeus,
that angel of music among angels,

that leading singer
on the steps of God's throne?
Do they still feel a trifle ashamed of it
before the world?
      — That I don't know. Perhaps.

And is life in Vienna still better
by two or three smiles
than anywhere else
      in the former monarchy?
Is Vienna still as velvety
as before?
      — No longer.

ADAGIO

Do you believe in dreams?
      — I've long stopped believing in them.
I too have woken from a dream
and walk on firm ground now.
      And yet!

What do the poets have to say about it?
      They only lie!
I once knew one of them.
He never dreamt of anything at night
and slept like a log.
But when he woke in the morning
and put on his slippers
he'd tell a dream of strangest beauty.

I sleep rather badly,
      and when I drop off
I find myself in the most strange surroundings.
Sometimes they frighten me
and even at best they are not agreeable.

Never have I in any dream of mine
walked among roses.
                    And yet!

But even so I'm grateful to the night
for those rare moments,
when in its quietude and in its darkness
I meet the dead
whom I loved in this life.

Why, even in our land
miracles sometimes still occur!

The dead arrive from God knows where
and there's no death between us.
But soon they leave again,
again for God knows where.
In vain do I call after them.

And standing once more right amongst us
is death.

TEMPO DI MINUETTO

And yet last night I dreamt
a beautiful dream.
At the depth of night there came a knock,
then silence,
as if my bedroom door
were not of wood
but of mute cotton-wool.
Even so I woke
and the visitor entered.

Do you know The Marriage of Figaro?
                    — But of course.
It was Cherubino!

I'm sure you know: this part
has to be sung by a girl,
and dressers in the dressing rooms
have a hard time
lacing those female breasts
into a boyish tunic,
so that their beauty should be noticed
as little as possible.

Signor Count Almaviva
notices nothing,
but I with great delight observe it all,
even though I often fear
those laces might break
as the singer sings
and has to draw breath.

And Cherubino sat down in my armchair
upon a styrofoam cushion
as lightly
        as a butterfly
on a silken flower.
A little puff of powder
tickled my nostrils.

Swear to me — he whispered,
bending over my face
so that he might talk in a whisper —
that with no single word will you betray
what I confide in you.

Willingly and at once I swore to him
and I felt sure
that I was perjuring myself.

The whole world believed
that Mozart's corpse
was flung in the Vienna cemetery
into a pauper's grave.

But Prague had loved him.
Thus he whose music
had entered under the roofs of this city
and who was happy here,
and happier still
when he crossed the familiar threshold,
is also buried here!

How lucky it is that even in our land
miracles sometimes still occur.

Mozart is not buried in capricious Vienna.
His grave is in Prague
on the Petřín hillside.

The grave by now is half-crumbled.
It's been a lot of years!
And no one knows about it.
At its head stands not a cross but
a jasmine shrub,
on the grave is a clump of blue violets.
And the grass all round is sprinkled
with gold.

ALLEGRO CON SPIRITO

His last words I no longer caught
as I opened my eyes.
At once I shut them tight again
to let the dream continue.
        But in vain.
Cherubino did not return.

I was up and about at an early hour
and hastened to the Petřín Hill.

The birds had all awoken
to finish their song
before the humans arrived.
But on the seats the morning dew
was still untouched.

I found the grave easily
by the violets.
Those golden drops
belonged to the poor primroses.

With my fingertips I touched the grass
and made small crosses,
the way that's customary when we wish
to greet one who is dead
and tell him something.

I know now why that nearby bench
          is such a favourite
especially with lovers
and why the birds at this spot
sing so jubilantly.

Below, Prague was beginning to awaken.
Mozart had loved her.
And just as pretty Lori lies at Mácha's feet
          so Prague
is lying at Mozart's.

VIEW FROM CHARLES BRIDGE

The rain had long since stopped.
In the pilgrimage church in Moravia,
where I had sought shelter from a storm,
they were chanting a Marian song
which stopped me from leaving.
I used to listen to it back home.

The priest had genuflected at the steps
and left the altar,
the organ had sobbed and fallen silent,
but the throng of pilgrims did not move.
Not until minutes later did the kneeling rise
and singing,
        without turning their heads,
all move backwards together
towards the open portals.

Never did I return there, never
again stand under the foliage of limes,
where the white banners waved
under the buzz of the bees.
I was homesick for Prague,
even though I'd only briefly stayed
outside her walls.

Day after day I gaze in gratitude
on the Castle of Prague
        and on its Cathedral:
I cannot tear my eyes away
from that picture.
        It is mine
and I also believe it is miraculous.

To me at least it assigned my destiny.
And as the twilight falls
        into Prague's windows
with stars in translucent darkness
I hear her ancient voice each time
and I hear poetry.
Without that voice I would be silent
as the bird
called the kiwi.

There are days when the Castle
        and its Cathedral
are gloomily magnificent,
when it seems
they were built of dismal rock
brought from the Moon.

An instant later, however, the towers of Prague
are once more wreathed in rays
        and roses
and that sweet delusion
of which love, too, is woven.

My frivolous steps along the streets,
my rose-red adventures
and loves and all the rest
are buried under light ash
since Time burnt down.

A few steps from the Royal Road
was a dark corner,
where tousle-haired prostitutes appeared
to walkers in the evenings,
luring into their dead wombs
young inexperienced boys,
as I was then.
Now all is silent there.
And only television aerials haunt
the ridges of the roofs.

But whenever I step on the pavement
of Charles Bridge
I am reminded of those pilgrims
in the pilgrimage church.

What bliss it is
        to walk upon this bridge!
Even though the picture is often glazed
by my own tears.

ALL THE BEAUTIES OF THE WORLD

A Selection from the Reminiscences

Translated by George Gibian

ON HIS PARENTS[1]

I know that nobody will ask me about this, that is obvious, but if it should interest somebody after all, and he were to ask me about the marriage of my parents, I would have to describe their marital union in contemporary terminology: it was the cohabitation of two individuals with different world views. My father was a Social Democrat, while my mother was a quiet, lyrical Catholic who obeyed divine and ecclesiastical laws as much as possible. She liked to go to church. It was a diversion from the stereotype of her week-days, from the mechanical sequence of daily work. It was her poetry. She went only rarely to communion — mostly when misfortunes occurred. She regarded them as God's punishment, and so she wanted to pacify the heavens.

My parents reacted to life differently, but in harmony, and not without self-sacrifice, and during the war not without going hungry. I remember well how my stomach used to growl. My mother surely had moments of contentment when she would throw herself on the cold, moist stones of the floor in the church in Žižkov, and tell the Virgin Mary openly about her troubles, trying, probably in vain, to hang a rosary made out of her tears on the Virgin's beautiful long hands. And I would walk back and forth between the two of them, from the Red Flag to "Thousandfold We Greet Thee", in a single day or evening. . . .

I should be lying if I complained. Their different world views did not cause me any special difficulties. I liked to go with my father to political meetings and popular assemblies, and liked equally well to go with my mother and sing long hymns about the Virgin Mary, standing by the stall where she was sitting.

Today when I stand above the urns of my parents, I must confess I loved my father more. My father was closer to me in the make-up of his character. Of course I loved my mother, but I catch myself thinking that what I felt was rather compassion for her bitter lot.

THE SCHOOLBOY AND THE PROSTITUTE

A friend who sat next to me in school told me about a little street in the Little Town section of Prague, which people call Corpses' Street, where there were several brothels. The girls were not allowed to go outside the houses at all, he said, and they were strictly guarded. Mainly, drunk Hungarian soldiers went there. The girls wore negligées and sat on the soldiers' knees, and the soldiers kissed them whenever they felt like it. That was all he knew. I promised him with a handshake I would not tell anybody.

Those were the last months of the First World War, and Prague was full of Hungarian soldiers.

As soon as I could, the next day, I went to the Little Town, partly out of curiosity, and partly for another reason. It is a long way from Žižkov. My heart beat furiously. At the market place several vegetable and fruit stands were still open. The butcher, who also had a shop in a house, was still selling at his stand in the street, where he had his butcher's block. A few pale white lambs hung in his small shop window, with pink bows around their slit throats. I loitered for a moment amidst the stands in the market and hesitated a little. Then I made a quick decision and went in the direction of the Corpses' Street, which was only a few steps away. I had a feeling I knew which street it was. I was right. The metal street sign said Břetislav Street, but as I later found out, nobody called it that. It was called Corpses' Street because funeral processions used to go up it to the cemetery on John's Hill. The street kept the name even after the cemetery had been abolished for a long time. It was a short, narrow street.

And deserted, not a person anywhere. I went up the little street close to the houses and looked with curiosity into the ground-floor windows. The smudged curtains did not move anywhere. So obviously the early afternoon was not the time of day for love. The girls were probably sleeping after lunch. At John's Hill I turned around, disappointed, and walked back. When I reached the last house at the bottom, I heard a soft knock on a window. I had to look in. The curtains parted, and a girl stood by the window with a dark braid hanging over her shoulder. Surprised, I remained stockstill.

When she saw my frightened look she smiled and said something to me, but I did not hear her voice through the glass. The street is so narrow that two steps were enough, and I was on the other side of the street. One can jump across it easily. Again, this time more calmly, I peered in the closed window. The girl was good-looking, at least I thought so. She was smiling at me so kindly that some of my fear left me. As soon as she realized that I was afraid and hesitating, she unbuttoned her white blouse in one movement. It seemed to me that I turned pale with fright, then immediately afterwards blood rushed forcefully into my head again. Terrified I looked into the window at the bared girlish breasts. I stood there confused, as if lightning had struck the pavement next to me. The girl continued smiling at me and I staggered. This lasted only a few seconds. The girl slowly buttoned up her blouse and with her hand beckoned me inside. Then the curtain closed again.

I fled in confusion.

I wanted to be alone. I rushed through Italian Street and stopped only at the end of the stairs in Seminary Gardens. The garden was in full bloom. How fortunate that the trees were blossoming just then. I felt comfortable under their blossom-wrapped branches. Beauty makes us feel at peace with the world. In the musical humming of bees I brought my thoughts in order a little, and I calmed down. I forced my heart to be quiet.

From my youth on, even before I had become quite aware of it, I belonged among the faithful believers in one of the most beautiful myths in the world. I believed in the myth of love of woman. Today it is hard to find. Women have thrown away their invisible halo, and therefore comb their hair differently. A pity. There is nothing more beautiful in the world than a naked flower and a naked woman. I know people are familiar with these beauties, but they are always mysterious to us, and we want to discover them again and again.

. . . .

The first vision of a woman's body which that dusty window on the ground floor held out to me slipped into my heart like a time bomb. I held its image, bright and shining, before my eyes. It was always with me, and for the time being it was what I desired most, when for the first time I began really to beg for love.

How chaste and maidenly blushing the two round blossoms seemed to me, in which a girl's body slowly blooms towards love, when the time of childhood is approaching the movable boundary of womanhood. I desired nothing else than to be able to lay my head between them and to press my mouth to that delight and to that odour. But fear tied my feet with an invisible rope . . . I did not dare enter the dark hallway leading to the girl. . . . In the end, however, I compelled myself to try. I decided firmly that I must take that couple of fateful steps. Desire forced me. After I had summoned my courage and pressed the door handle, everything would be easy. Only those couple of steps. I will shut my eyes and clench my teeth. It will take only a few seconds. With this resolution, I returned to the house. In the doorway, however, I found a strange old woman. She noticed my fear and hesitation right away and caught me by the sleeve to pull me inside. With her toothless mouth she whispered something lascivious about the beautiful girls inside who were waiting for me to choose one of them. I tore myself from her and rushed away again.

I did not go to the Little Town for several days. And then I again took an oath that I would conquer my weakling's fear, my cowardice. But this time, as soon as I entered the street, in front of the house towards which I was walking, I saw a fat rat on the pavement. It was dragging something dirty in its mouth. It noticed me immediately, but stopped calmly, and looked at me slowly with its pink eyes. After a while it slunk across the stone threshold and vanished in the hallway which I might have entered myself. I turned away in disgust and never again returned to that street. I was convinced for a long time that never again in my life would such happiness await me and that never again should I see anything so miraculously surprising as I did that beautiful day in the dusty window in sad Corpses' Street in the Little Town, when almost all the trees were blooming in April in the old Seminary Park and the weather was so fine.

What a fool I was.

Often when I recalled that adventure, I sighed — how could I have been so mistaken, how could I have been so mistaken.

HOW I BECAME A POET[1]

The first publication of Ivan Suk's poems (by S.K. Neumann in *June*) woke me out of the dream in which my desire and determination to become a poet had been lulled to sleep. Jealousy possessed me. It never occurred to us that *June* was a magazine which would print our little poems.

When Suk arrived with a copy of the magazine and even showed us his fee, I could hardly keep myself from showing my impotent envy. For several days I walked around all alone, making speeches to myself full of tears and despair. A hundred times I picked up paper and pencil, and a hundred times I put them down, overcome by impotence.

When Suk published more poems in Hora's Saturday supplement to *Právo Lidu* (a Socialist newspaper), my sadness and powerlessness increased still further. A while later, when the first witty and amusing poems by Němec also appeared in *June*, I decided that whatever the cost, despite everything, I must write some poetry.

It was a long night. I tore a mountain of paper into shreds which I immediately threw into the stove to be rid of the nonsense I had written. I wrote verses about every possible thing: love, Prague, the cemetery, life — some cheerful, others sad, some tragic, others comic — but they all burned in the fire in a few seconds. Finally, when I could no longer think up anything at all, I wrote about the things which were in front of my eyes: the windows, the stove, the bed. The poem about my bed turned out so well that I sent it to Hora. I compared my bed to a mule walking up a narrow trail towards the stars, in the Nevada mountains.

Hora sent me word by return mail that I was an idiot and that I should stop writing immediately. I was completely demolished. I crawled into a hole and seeing no other way out, threw myself at my textbooks, which till then I had neglected with a contemptuous smile, thinking I was a poet.

I decided to become a scholar: perhaps a mathematician, or a historian. Or maybe even a biologist? The upshot of it all was that I thought of myself as an ugly hunchback who had fallen in love with a queen, saw her all the time in his dreams, and wept. Meanwhile Němec and Suk climbed from one success to another. Suk was already putting together his first book for Minařík's publishing house, and around the dusty hat of Němec, young, genuine laurels of poetry were winding themselves.

After the ointment of resignation had somewhat cured my wound, I found consolation in my algebra and geometry classes. Not that I understood those fields of knowledge very well; I didn't, but they were the subjects which reminded me least of my sad catastrophe. How could I have chosen Greek or Latin, when Catullus's pleasing poems continually evoked in me the desperate night that I spent over sheets of white paper which I doggedly defaced with my lyrical banalities. Even the flying swallow and the velvety bat in the zoology textbook and the pictures of blossoms with cross-sections of seed pods and petals were so lyrical that they forced me to think of poetical evenings and the spring which just then was filling the whole town with light and fragrance.

At that time I used to carry a heavy walking stick, and I took up smoking cigars, because both of those affectations were characteristic of our maths teacher. I slouched when I walked and I dressed carelessly, because that too was typical of that sloppy teacher.

Have you ever seen spring on Petřín Mountain? It is amazing. Hardly has the snow disappeared, gurgling hurriedly along the paths leading steeply downhill, when the cherry trees in the Strahov gardens burst into bloom. To walk down the middle of the park on a beautiful day and to reflect stubbornly on the principles of equations seemed to me a very appropriate protest against the poetry that I hated. The blossoms of the golden rain tree poured from the low branches behind the blouses of some girls sitting on benches and reading Mácha's *May*, but this couldn't shake my conviction that love which was so closely connected with lyrical yearning must be resisted with the elevated, superior, haughty cynicism of a Peruvian executioner.

Prague looked like a chess board at the beginning of a game. The king and queen stood over there, here was the golden rook. The apartment houses and villas were the pawns. My weak cigars slowly drugged my eyes. Without knowing just how it happened, I found myself on the small observation platform on Hunger Wall. The chessmen on the board moved slowly and deliberately before my eyes. On the horizon stood the frostbitten tower of the Žižkov church. The dial of its clock glittered fiercely.

The alpha, beta, gamma, delta of angles, the infinity of the circle, and the alphabet of algebraic paradigms at that moment lost something of their urgency. It seemed as if the pigeons which were flying around loudly clapping their wings had eaten up the pygmy letters in my hands. I sat down on a round stone which had the four points of the compass and the names of Europe's cities inlaid in gold. Paris to the West, followed by London, Bremen, Hamburg, Leipzig, Berlin, Bucharest, Budapest, Milan, Genoa, Monte Carlo, Nice.

It was the rose of Europe.

At that moment is seemed to me that I was holding Europe in my hands, that I was lifting it to my lips and nostrils, that I was smelling the perfume of remote distances and the perfume of the world. Clouds, awesomely beautiful clouds, sailed above Prague, and the perfume of spring excited the centres of my thought. The glory of the town lay at my feet. I savoured thoroughly the dramatic day on this relief map, tied like a knot, and looking like a massive, stone stage prop. Gold and kisses. Women in front of mirrors. Treason and love. Heroism and roses. Passions and deaths.

No, it was impossible to be a mathematician.

Well, boy, dip the pen once more into the cerulean blue of the sky and write, even if only on the cuff of your sleeve. Try one more time to be a poet. Write something about the beauties which pass before your eyes, as you lie on this stone which lets you sense the hitherto unknown beauty of the world. Strew the dust of stars on your writings so that they will dry, and you will see what happens.

That evening I wrote a poem and, with a pounding heart, sent it to Hora.

He printed it the next day.

With my poem on the table in front of me, I wrote another with miraculous ease and sent it to Neumann. It came out in the next issue of *June*.

When Neumann gave me his hand, I was afraid to shake it. It seemed too great a happiness for me. And when he even invited me to have lunch with him, my knees shook and I was not able to swallow the food.

Neumann's friendly reception gave me courage, and I decided to go to see Hora, with a new little poem written in beautiful calligraphy. Phlegmatic, wearing glasses, his eyes eternally glazed, Hora received me rather coldly. He seemed to be of the opinion that a little poem is no great event, particularly when it was written by a twenty-year-old man.

After these successes I looked up Němec and Suk. By that time I was able to look them calmly in the eyes. I walked with them into the centre of Prague, stepping lightly, talking about poetry.

By the end of the school year I had failed maths hopelessly.

It was more than half a century ago that, not without some hesitation, Karel Teige knocked on the door of the then small publishing house, in order to offer Václav Petr the manuscript of my third book, *On the Waves of TSF*. At that time radio did not yet exist in our country, and as there was not even a word for it, we used the French initials for telegraphy without wire (*telegraphie sans fil*).

Our hesitation was not groundless. The book was really unusual for those days. Take, for example, the title. It was one of the first books to proclaim allegiance to the new directions in art. I as its author, and also Teige, who designed the typography, both did all that was in our power to proclaim loudly the spirit of poetism on its pages, with provocative oddities. Some poems contained slight blasphemies against serious things, and in addition to serious poems, there were others marked by the inversion of Mácha's motto:

Light sorrow on the face
deep laughter in the heart.[1]

We hoped that the publisher would at least be surprised, if not altogether reluctant to publish such an unusual book. He surprised us. He looked over the manuscript, agreed to everything, accepted the manuscript and two or three months later, the book came out exactly the way we had wanted.

Teige had made heroic efforts. The print shop of Mr Obzina in Vyskov had to use almost all the typefaces in their founts to set the book, and they had to discard all the classical rules of typography which had been followed and perfected since the times of Gutenberg until the modern standards of book design had been achieved. The titles and the texts of the poems were in the most varied type faces. Every poem was set differently. Some pages were horizontal, others vertical. The old printer in Vyskov shook his head over this manner of doing things, but he let us have our way. Today young people would call Teige's design a typographical rodeo.

The readers were most amused by the short poem, "Abacus of Love":

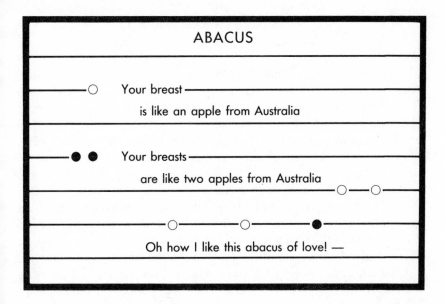

ABACUS

○ Your breast
is like an apple from Australia

● ● Your breasts
are like two apples from Australia ○ — ○

○ ○ ●
Oh how I like this abacus of love! —

The poem, if one can even call it a poem, was set in the typographic image of a child's abacus. But I must add a brief explanation to these verses. In those days, delicatessen stores really sold Australian apples in the winter. The apples did not have a very pronounced taste, because they ripened only while they were being shipped. But they were very beautiful. Each apple was wrapped in fine silk paper, and Mr Paukert, the delicatessen store owner on National Street, placed them on a platter in the window of the store, each one unwrapped a little bit, so that people could see their unusually beautiful colouring. They were rare and expensive. But that has nothing to do with my poem.

That book which today already belongs to history was supposed to be republished in a facsimile edition some time ago. It did not work out. A pity.

So, Mr Petr, across the precipice of time and life, I offer you my hand. We are both old now. But how pleasant it is to remember the times when one was young, when one took pleasure in everything new, did not think about death, and was not afraid of anything.

ON HAŠEK, THE AUTHOR OF
THE GOOD SOLDIER ŠVEJK

The war was over and Jaroslav Hašek moved in at the Sauers' soon after his return with his second wife, whom he brought with him from Russia. The eternal mystificator pretended she was a duchess. She didn't look like it. We could see directly into their window and we could watch their levée late in the morning. Afterwards Mrs Šura, as her Žižkov neighbours called her, liked to observe life in our busy street. . . .

Jaroslav Hašek sometimes came to our pub. He would not stay long. There he was too near to his wife, who vainly attempted to make Hašek stay at home. When someone once asked him why he didn't come to the Golden Angel pub, he said that there were stairs there. Indeed, there are three little steps leading into the tavern.

One summer evening he came into our tavern dressed as if he were at home. He was in short sleeves, wore slippers, and held up his trousers with his hand. He confessed that Šura had locked up his shoes, braces and coat. He was only on his way to the pharmacy. His wife was sick and the doctor had given her a prescription. In order not to be making a trip for nothing, he brought along a jug. Before the tavern keeper had filled his jug and before he had drunk a glass of beer at the counter, he played pool with us. He played miserably. When he finished his third glass, he decided he had to go fetch the medicine. His wife was waiting, and he said he would stop by to pick up the jug on his way back from the pharmacy. He didn't come.

Two days later someone knocked sharply on the door of our apartment. A furious Šura stood in the doorway and demanded angrily: "Where is Jaroušek?"

Then she cried a little, talked to my mother, and left, wiping her tears.

No, Hašek had not met any Rimbaud, he had not gone abroad either. He came back a week later, with a jug of beer but without any medicine. After all, the medicine was not needed any longer. His wife was in good health again. Too much so, he laughed.

During his long journey, in shirtsleeves, wearing slippers in summery Prague, in all sorts of taverns, amongst friends and companions who made no attempt to show respect for his work, Hašek had written a whole instalment of *The Good Soldier Švejk*. He would write on the corner of a table, and when he had finished a few pages, one of his pals would take the manuscript directly to the publisher, Synek, who would pay out an appropriate amount for the work done. Not a crown more, of course. So one day and one evening were taken care of; then the next day he would have to write again, if he didn't want to sit over an empty glass.

Given this method of writing, one must ask, of course, how the book would have turned out if he had written it in peace and comfort at a desk. But that is the eternal, fateful "if". Maybe if Hašek had not written on beer bespattered tables, in the noise of pub talk, among thirsty friends, because he needed a few ten-crown notes for beer, perhaps the book would never have been written, and Hašek would not be the Hašek whose name became famous all over Europe.

Hašek, as you know, died shortly afterwards. Mrs Šura died too. Hašek's faithful friend and patient companion František Sauer died too. Only Švejk, the pyknic, extrovert and cyclothenic, with an absolute sense for unadorned reality, as Professor Vondráček characterized him, goes on living merrily not only in the book, but wandering all over the world, to places where he never meant to go.

A DAY IN THE COUNTRY

It was June. Farmers were mowing hay. The previous evening we had been in Náchod, where Píša gave a lecture and local actors read poetry. In the morning we took a bus to the valley of Ratibořice. As you know that is quite far.

I am a city person. I was born in the city and I have spent all my life in the city. When I was sick and took the cure in a tiny watering place, called Dubí, at the edge of the Krušné Mountains, I would take a commuter tram to Teplice almost every day to get black coffee in a coffeehouse. "It's not the coffee you wanted," Píša used to laugh, "you had that in Dubí, but you missed the smell of sewers."

Píša was a country person. He was born in a small town in Southern Bohemia and he was happy in the fields and under green trees. He loved Kinsky Park. When the park was in blossom, he tried to drop in for at least a couple of minutes. Whenever he had a chance, he took walks in Kampa, and called a short route through the quiet Kampa "Píša's Path". He went to the coffeehouse, in which I spent many beautiful spring and summer days, only at night, sometimes after an evening performance.

In Grandmother's Valley, however, even I spent a few dazzling moments, which one apparently can experience only in this country and in this region, hallowed by the reality which we respect and the legends which we love.

That morning, a delightful day offered itself to us. The little Ratibořice chateau in the distance radiated so much artistic colourfulness that it reminded us of the best etchings by Mr Vincent Mortstadt, who was skilful enough not to omit a single beautiful detail. In a remote valley people were mowing hay, and when the warm wind was blowing gently, we smelled the mingled odours of hay, of freshly cut grass, and of the ripe meadow, from which the sun was drinking morning dew and all the hidden nectars. As we walked slowly along the meadow path, our eyes could not absorb all the colours, the white and yellow daisies, the blue veil of sage and the red poppy. There was also the tenderly pink sainfoin, not to speak of all the constantly shifting and trembling greens.

The meadow path itself was overgrown with a mat of flattened grasses and was bordered by wild thyme and the quiet weeping of dark red tearflowers, without which no summer day exists. . . .

We glimpsed a tiny little girl, with sunburned feet, running through tall grass. She is running, she is hurrying, she tosses her

162

pigtail over her shoulder and her shining eyes are filled with that radiance seen only in children's eyes. She runs past us, perhaps she is talking to herself; she passes us as if we were not on the path. We felt like stroking the perfumed air which her unexpected appearance stirred up, we wanted to stroke the meadow through which she had run, and the path trodden by her tiny girl's feet. We saw her feet clearly when they sped past us and accidentally snagged a chicory blossom, which stuck between her toes and looked like a precious stone, which a beautiful princess in the days of yore would place on her big toe.

ON TEIGE:
A DANSE MACABRE IN SMÍCHOV

Men understand many things, we could even say everything. They master complicated machines and bend over a computer with less hesitation than a typist over a typewriter. But often, when they come near a woman, it happens that they don't understand her at all. I know, you will say that a woman is not a machine. Of course she isn't, but even so, some men calculate astonishingly well the deviations in the paths of invisible or imperceptible stars, but they don't understand the women whom they meet every day in their orbits. . . . The thing that is special and unique in the behaviour and gestures of women simply eludes them.

Even some writers have been like this. They speak convincingly about women's souls in the pages of their books, because they understand psychology well, but they let their own marriages become pitifully shipwrecked through their own fault. This is true of famous, renowned writers. The ones who walk in the gardens of philosophy are the worst.

It is as though the seductive mystery of a woman were a mystery. Or is it?

I want to talk about the death of Karel Teige, though quite inappropriately, I have started almost from the end. One must start telling a story from the very beginning. Teige himself demands that.

When Teige and I decided that we would take our first trip to Paris, he persuaded me to have a tailor make us nice new suits so that we would make a good showing for our country, which nobody was asking of us, and also so that we would make a good showing for our modern art, and that was something we ourselves wanted. In Prague we walked around dressed any old way.

Teige knew a tailor on National Street in Prague, Mr Turek, who had a shop over the former Union Coffeehouse. He was not just an ordinary tailor, and he was not inexpensive. I had very little money so I hesitated, but in the end gave in. Mr Turek picked a grey English cloth called pepper and salt, and our suits were soon finished. Two weeks later we were wearing them down the boulevards, with "enchantingly rained on" hats, as Milena Jesenská, then still a fashion reporter, used to say.

The Eiffel Tower, which we had invoked rather piously, stared at us indifferently.

In Paris it is beautiful even when it is raining, and all the more when the weather is fine. It was a perfumed summer day, and we had a date with the painter Šíma. We were looking for Rue Segnier 14, when a most beautiful young woman slid out of a car in front of us. An elegant woman, of course. She looked as if she were cut out from a novel by Colette. Her veil did not hide her eyes, and glittering gold bracelets jingled on her wrist. She shimmered past us in cloudlets of perfume, and we were so enchanted that we stopped and looked at one another.

"Too bad I don't have the time, I would have talked her into becoming my girl friend," Teige said suddenly.

It surprised me a little, but Teige said it so matter-of-factly that I said nothing. We never interfered with one another in such things, anyway.

Today, fifty years later, I realize that I shouldn't have been surprised. Teige was right. A man is a man and should always aim higher than he can reach. Only in that way do beautiful and interesting unhappy loves come into being, loves which readers like to hear about.

Good-bye Paris. You will never again be so beautiful.

When we came back to Prague, we were about twenty-five, and enthusiasm was in our eyes. And longings in our hearts! It is a pity that then we were only slightly conscious of our happiness. Unfortunately one only finds out when it is too late.

Devětsil was expanding; new members were joining.[1] Thus it surprised us all the more when Teige began to skip the meetings at the Slavia coffeehouse. He came irregularly and left without a trace. In the evening he did not even talk us into going to bars where saxophones moaned seductively and dancing girls offered their arms.

Toyen — at that time we still called her Manka — accused Teige bluntly: "You have fallen in love, right?"

Teige, with some hesitation, admitted it. From his youth, Teige had preached the right to free love. Marriage was a bourgeois relic.

In those days we once caught a glimpse of Nezval in the street carrying an ironing board to his home. Apparently they had not let him in the streetcar with it. He held it like a guitar, and he looked quite funny. Toyen burst out laughing, and Teige was bitterly ironic. Nezval, all red, was embarrassed.

After that, life moved on, raced, roared, passed. Every day we died a little, as Tristan Tzara counselled, but nobody reflected about time. We published book after book; we had pockets full of poems. We wanted to "astound the bourgeoisie", but it seems we

165

astounded them only mildly. They were not at all afraid of us.

In 1929 seven writers signed a manifesto. I was the youngest of the seven. My friends Teige, Nezval, Halas, Píša and still other authors issued a counter-manifesto, and after a motion by Julius Fučík, I was expelled from *Devětsil*.

But by that time, it did not hurt me very much. *Devětsil* was coming to the end of its creative mission in Czech cultural life, and its beautiful and rich history was drawing to a close.

Its members no longer needed the young association which had helped them in their work. Many of the issues which concerned the avant garde generation had been decided, and each of us was already mature enough to go his own way and to want not to be shackled by the rules of the game, which we had invented for *Devětsil* and which Teige had enforced fairly severely.

Then our women began to interfere directly or indirectly with our regular meetings, and so there were more and more empty seats around the table.

You know how it goes. If they want to, women can turn an empire upside down, how much more easily an association of artists. But it wasn't the women who subverted the pleasant friendships of our young association, not the women.

Nezval in his memoirs relates how, evening after evening, after I had said good-bye to my girl, I hurried, late, to where I thought my friends might be. Yes, he was right, it was like that. But I mostly wanted to see Teige, with whom I always needed to talk. He was an untiring, helpful adviser and friend.

What hurt me most about the *Devětsil* split was the damage it did to my friendship with Teige. We saw one another less and less often, although at first we both made an effort not to let that happen. But when Nezval and Teige imported surrealism from Paris later on, I began to see them less and less. They made new friendships with French artists, and Nezval, with his brutal robustness, threw himself into the mainstream of the new movement. Teige, in addition to his interest in surrealism, concentrated his interest on modern architecture.

. . . In time *Devětsil* became for me a dear but slightly bitter memory from the past.

[Teige] had gradually opened up the world of modern art for me, a world which I had not known, and with my poor knowledge of languages could not know. I liked poetry, but Teige taught me to love it, and the plastic arts as well. He taught me how to look at modern paintings and sculptures. And he taught me the caution which is necessary in the world of art. Not everything that calls itself art is art, nor everything that people hold out to us and sometimes force on us.

Teige did not succeed with me in one thing only. He persistently but vainly tried to talk me into learning how to dance. He even offered to teach me himself. Nezval was supposed to play the piano for these dance lessons.

Teige liked to dance with complete absorption. In his library he had pinned up a title page of the old *L'Illustration* with a charming drawing by Gaverni, on which a very young girl, who had just returned from a ball and was still wearing her gown, had fallen asleep on top of a table. Under the drawing were the slightly altered words of Jesus Christ: Much will be forgiven her, for she has danced much. . . .

Teige used to sit somewhat uncomfortably in his study. He would tuck in his legs and sit down on top of them in a chair. He would read and immediately translate for us the poems of Apollinaire. In this way we became acquainted not only with *Alcools* and *Caligrammes*, but also with the poems of Jacob, Cocteau, Cendrars, Reverdy, and other modern poets. Vildrac's beautiful *Book of Love*, which we had loved before that, receded into the background, because Cubism, Futurism, and Tzara's Dada rushed towards us, thanks to Teige.

At Topič's bookshop Teige bought all the monographs on modern art. And so we came to know Picasso and Bracque and all the noteworthy figures of French and Italian modern art.

Marinetti came to Teige's study when he was visiting Prague. He boasted that he had inherited seven brothels in Cairo, from some relative. They were very profitable. He claimed that he financed the Futurist movement in Italy with his earnings. He recited his *Liberated Words* for us, too. When he was reciting, he would walk up and down the room, waving his arms, jumping up and squatting down. He was a very vivacious and likeable Italian. He admired the Czech language. It was the only language in which Marinetti had several names. Once he heard someone say distinctly "Marinettiho" (the accusative of Marinetti, in the Czech declension), another time "Marinettimu" (the dative ending). He liked that, it didn't exist in any other language. But he became sadly notorious in the Abyssinian War. He dropped out of our hearts.

Teige died on October 1, 1951. It was a mournful autumn day. The electrocardiogram had lied. The doctor who read the instrument shortly before Teige's death could only conclude that his heart was functioning normally. It was not. It had not functioned normally for a long time. Teige's heart was so worn out that the doctor performing the autopsy could not believe that he had been able to live for such a long time with this heart.

His death was the consequence of intensive work which literally did not let him sleep. He worked all night. In the evening after ten o'clock he would sit down at his desk at home and work till the following dawn. Necessity made him hurry. He was afraid he would not finish his books. At that time he was being systematically attacked by fierce and unjust critics in the Prague press. Because he had been quite defenceless, many rumours started after his death, induced also by the silence which suddenly enveloped his death, his name, and of course his books, too.

André Breton in his monograph about the painter Toyen related one of these rumours as if it had really happened: he said that Karel Teige immediately took poison when he was arrested, and that his wife killed herself right afterwards by jumping out the window. It must be stated that Teige was neither arrested nor interrogated.

The events, equally dramatic, were different.

There are women, and they are usually younger women, but sometimes also older ones, who, if a misfortune happens and their husband dies, come home from the funeral and cry. They cry for several days. Then they dry their tears, powder their noses, and look around at the world. No, I am not reproaching them. Such is life. I'm on the women's side.

The marvellous French poet Alfred de Vigny, well acquainted with a shaky marriage, said about women that they were the destroyers of passions. Not all of them! Our Petr Bezruč liked to quote this aphorism about women: A mother is the only woman who loves a man selflessly. He added that the French say that, and that they definitely know women. But it is not always true.

I will not let anyone take away from me the myth of woman, with which men since time immemorial have crowned woman's beauty. Neither old age, nor sickness, nor pain, nor even disappointment, which usually is the worst, will deprive my old eyes of this beautiful view of woman. I am an inveterate feminist. I defend women even though today they do not need it any longer. They defend themselves very well on their own.

These few sentences about women are a prologue. The curtain goes up, and on the stage stand a husband and wife. Someone knocks and another woman enters. No, for God's sake, it is not the beginning of a comedy about marriage, such as we know by the dozen in the theatre. On the contrary, here begins a unique plot: a tragedy of a man and of two women's hearts.

"As you certainly know," Teige's young friend Vratislav Effenberger wrote me, "Karel Teige in his romanticism was captivated by free love. He loved his wife sincerely. And when at the beginning of the war he met Miss E, he tried to prove to himself and to the two women that their relationship could be happy and harmonious."

I knew about Teige's new relationship. I had known his wife when I was young. She was a serious, attractive, rare woman. His friend I had only met fleetingly once at Girgal's. She too was an unusual woman; she also was attractive and certainly interesting. At one of these meetings he invited me warmly to come to see him at his Smíchov Šalamounka place. It was not long before his death. How I regret that I did not immediately accept his invitation. Soon it was too late.

I never doubted that he had a serious relationship with both women. He did not want to be, and of course also could not be, the participant in a banal marital triangle. But I am surprised that this unusually bright and intelligent person could believe that he would create a calm and harmonious relationship with two women. How could he not know that in the area of true love no such thing is possible between women. He could love both women sincerely himself, but women, if they love, are not able to share their love. This weighed on him like a heavy burden and cost him continual heavy exhaustion. That too did not add any strength to his weary, sick heart. Evidently all three suffered from the situation.

Every evening Teige worked at home. Only towards dawn would he go to bed and sleep during the morning. At noon he went to visit his friend. She lived near Arbes Square in Smíchov. There he ate lunch and in the afternoon Miss E helped him with quotations for his book. So the days passed, and three years went by, from 1949 till October 1951.

On the fateful October day, because he was late, Miss E decided she would go to meet him. She waited in vain. They passed each other on the way. Only when she was returning home did she find him in the streetcar shelter at Arbes Square. He was leaning against the aluminium pillar, and he called to her. His face was painfully distorted. It was a face already marked by death. She moved him with difficulty to her apartment. Walking was torture for him. Once in the apartment, he sat down. He felt terribly sick. She hurried to get a doctor. It was a while before she found one. When she returned, Teige was dead.

Without hesitation, she decided she would also die. First, though, she had to give the news of Teige's death to his wife. She wrote a letter: "Karel is no more. He died today at noon." And she sent it to Šalamounka by a taxidriver.

As soon as his wife read the note, she immediately burned all of Teige's correspondence. There was a lot of it. Although he saw both women every day, he wrote letters to each of them almost every day. After this sad ceremony she killed herself with gas.

Miss E. lived for only a few days. She used the time to put in order the manuscripts which Teige had left at her place and gave them to friends. Then she followed Teige's wife. She turned on the gas valve.

With her dying, this sorrowful dance of death ended. The public learned nothing about it "thanks" to measures taken after Teige's death.

We lived in the presence of a beautiful and extraordinary person and writer. What strengths his rich personality radiated!

After Teige's funeral, the ceremonial hall was almost empty. Only a few of his young friends, whom I had not yet met, were present. Of his friends and acquaintances of our generation — the generation of Teige, not of Wolker, as the phrase has already become established — there was nobody. His faithful Muzika, the painter, and I stood alone behind the empty chairs.

A FEW MINUTES BEFORE EXECUTION: May 1945

There surely does not exist a single biography of F.M. Dostoevsky anywhere in the world which does not describe how Dostoevsky was sentenced to death and how he felt during those moments when he was face to face with death. That is obvious. Who would fail to remember the description of those overwhelming minutes when the condemned prisoners, including Dostoevsky, were taken to Semyonov Square in Petersburg and in the last seconds the Tsar granted them mercy. What a horrifying and earthshaking moment for the author, a literary genius who knew how to lay bare the human soul and to penetrate to the very bottom of human passions in turmoil.

Dostoevsky, however, writes about that climactic moment of his life surprisingly simply. In later letters from Siberia, where he was sent after he was pardoned, he wrote to his brother many angry letters in which he described in detail all the cruelties which the prisoners suffered but which are really not the same as the terror of immediate death. However, he wrote on the whole calmly and simply about those few minutes. "They dressed us in white execution clothes, and tied us in threes to the posts." In the last moments Dostoevsky was able to embrace his colleagues. Then they let the prisoners kiss a cross, and finally swords were broken over their heads, because they were noblemen.[1] In the very last seconds he became aware how much he loved his brother. That is all. He described it as concisely and calmly as I am writing it myself.

May 1945 found several editors, employees, and officials of the administration at the People's House on Hybernská Street, where we were already planning a new, liberated daily Social-Democratic newspaper.[2] Others were working alongside us on the first number of the new liberated, no longer illegal, Red Right (a Communist newspaper). On Saturday, May 5, people began to tear down German shop signs in the streets of Prague, and arrest Nazi soldiers. The Prague Uprising had begun. We stayed in the editorial offices. Others joined us: typesetters, layout men and staff. Other editors also hurried to join us and we immediately started to work. Soon the presses began to hum, and paperboys distributed the first copies in town. When the first shots were fired in the street, even some passersby, who could no longer run across the street towards either Žižkov or the Powder Tower, took shelter in the People's House. The Czechoslovak flag and the red flag waved on the People's House building. Chestnut trees blossomed in the garden of the house. Amidst the chestnut trees there also grew a *gingko biloba*, a rather rare tree in our country, a relic of the times when the palace belonged to the Kinskýs and possessed an aristocratic garden.

The Masaryk Railroad Station was occupied by the Czechs, and the Germans shelled it. A shell hit the People's House, too, and shell fragments and bullets flew around the courtyard. Because the Germans fortified themselves not only in the YMCA at Poříč but also next door in the Anglobank, shots whistled over our typewriters and over the hairdos of our typists. We moved the entire editorial office downstairs into the basement, where the presses were, and then still further down, to the paper storeroom. I wrote verses about May on rolls of newsprint in the storeroom. It was a good way to write. It went well. Who needs desks! Nights flowed into days. Dramatic days went by. Saturday, Sunday, Monday, Tuesday.

The Czech unit which was assigned to the People's House by the Revolutionary Command Post was small and poorly armed. They had seized some weapons when they disarmed the German soldiers who had been occupying the Monopol Hotel across from the railroad station. However, the situation changed quickly to our disadvantage. The Germans took the Masaryk Station and shot everybody they found there. Only a few people saved themselves, at the last moment, in the People's House, unarmed. After that things happened quickly. The Germans captured the corner house at Havlíček Street. There in the delicatessen they found stores of wine and champagne. Because the walls between the cellars had previously been broken through to link the buildings, on German orders, the German troops found themselves in the People's House, and the tiny Czech unit divided itself between the cellar and the main entrance. The Germans came to the House in an armoured car. One of the defenders in the cellar used his rifle to shoot the first soldier who came through. The soldier dropped immediately in front of me, and I had my first opportunity to see how death looks from close up. Lying on the ground, he still called to his comrades to shoot, but he himself could not even raise his rifle. He did not even have the strength to pull the trigger of his rifle which lay on the ground. That is how quickly life escaped through the wound in his stomach.

For a confused minute we trampled around in his blood, but a

German officer appeared in the gap in the wall and ordered us to raise our hands. He had the women stay in the cellar and ordered the men to leave through the rear exit to Havlíček Street and go into the vestibule of the burning Masaryk Station. The soldiers who escorted us assured us with a smile that at the railway station we would immediately be shot. First we had to sit down on the tracks. A few steps away from us was a pile of dead Czechs who had been shot a moment before. We were only waiting for a long hospital train which stood on the tracks behind us to leave.

The train was full of badly wounded people lying on cots, one on top of the other. The Germans shot a boy before our eyes, on the spur of the moment — an ancient Austrian bayonet unfortunately happened to stick out from under his coat — and then they shot an older man, because some German soldiers said that they had seen him firing. Both were shot with a revolver in the back of their necks. When blood spurts from a hole in the nape of the neck, it is not a pretty sight. The old man was silent, but the boy whined pitifully before his death.

I don't know why, but probably because they could not get the hospital train to leave the station quickly enough, and because the fire in the station was spreading fast, they ordered us to get up and led us in twos to Žižkov. The heat of the fire was so fierce that we had to protect our faces with handkerchiefs. . . .

How often I used to run happy and content on this street above the station, from my earliest childhood on. This was where I used to hurry when I was happily leaving for all my vacations in Kralupy, and where I returned into my mother's arms. And now we were walking there in silence, full of fear, not knowing what was ahead of us.

At the George of Padĕbrady barracks they stood us against the wall, and we waited again. They told us one more time that we were going to be shot, in the courtyard of the barracks. But in the courtyard the Germans were preparing their flight from Prague and their preparations were not yet finished.

When we had walked along Hrabovka Street, the spring breezes were filled with the scent of lilacs from the park on Vítkov Hill, where I once spent days and evenings wandering above the smoke of the railway station, my fingers interlaced with a girl's, my mood one of innocent joy, my laughter carefree. I remembered clearly the summer violets, whose scent never satiates me, even today. The lookout pavilion, which still exists today, offers one of the most beautiful views in Prague, although it is sometimes a little

173

smoky because of the locomotives at the station under the hill.

Negotiators carrying white flags on their shoulders passed the barracks in the middle of the street twice, coming and going. They did not even look at us. We did not have an inkling what they were doing, or what issues were involved in their negotiations, which lasted quite a long time.[3] We experienced tense moments until at the last minute the Germans decided to exchange us for a group of German women, children and old men, whom our people had caught as they were fleeing. I had no idea how long we had stood at the wall of the barracks. A German soldier had pulled my watch off my wrist when we were walking up from the People's House. But it seemed like eternity to me.

The Germans gave us a sharp command to scatter in all directions. After a long walk past the barricades, Píša and I and two others found ourselves at Troja Bridge. There we slept in a friend's house through the last stormy night. From the windows of the apartment house, which in those days stood there almost alone, we looked at Schornhorst's unit, some of whose troops occupied the road sloping down from Bulovka to Troja Bridge. The unit's assignment was to destroy the town and flee into American captivity. In the first task fortunately they did not succeed. In the second, only partly. But that is well-known history.

Aware of the impossibility of comparing a world-famous genius with a lyrical poet from a small country, still I used to envy Dostoevsky's unique experience: to be sentenced to death, to come to know the moment when one must necessarily leave his life, accept that inexorable fact, and then to be saved and to taste again the security and the sweetness of life, to experience that couple of terrible minutes when time is quickly pulling one towards annihilation, and then to gaze at the broad expanse of time, which lies ahead like a beautiful landscape. What drama must run through a person's mind in those few minutes! What does such a moment mean to someone, especially to a writer, who has the ability to articulate such an experience accurately?

Without comparing anything except just this human event, I should like to say this on my own behalf:

When Píša and I stood by the wall of the Karlin barracks, I pulled out of my pocket a piece of bread and cheese, which I had taken from the German supplies when I was leaving the Hotel Monopol. Neither the bread nor the cheese were fresh any more, but we ate them hungrily. Then I thought of my family at home. I knew that on the whole they were safe. Yet somehow in my subconscious I did not at all admit the idea that I should not see them again. I chased this from my thoughts decisively. I looked at the sad, ugly houses across from me. All the windows were shut, apparently out of caution. Once in a while a curtain was pulled aside somewhere and a face appeared. Then near the Karlín overpass I noticed a metal sidewalk toilet, which awakened a grotesque memory.

Many years before, an unknown, but obviously quite skilled painter had painted on that toilet wall, with tar, a naked woman, in a most risqué position. When we were boys, we often came to look at this picture. It was there for quite a long time. It excited us. For boys it was quite an extraordinary experience. While we were standing by the barracks, that picture appeared clearly before my mind's eye, although until then I had almost forgotten that rather inelegant artifact.

I looked again at the grey windows across the street. Smoke came out of the small chimneys. I wondered, what are those happy people cooking for lunch today? They did not have to stand by the wall of the barracks; they only looked out at us from time to time through the curtains. Please, for goodness sake, do not take this to be bold courage, but in those moments I really did not think about death, although death was waiting for us a few steps away in the courtyard, and we already somehow took that fact for granted.

When they scattered us in all directions and we breathed the sweet air of freedom and heard the Prague radio announce in loud tones that the Germans had surrendered, I can say that then we immediately forgot the hours we had lived through.

And years later?

Recently I happened to be in those exact places where we survived those very difficult moments, and I did not remember them at all. Only after I returned home, did I realize I had walked through those places and had not been aware of it.

Today I do not remember those terrible moments any more than a child running after a new ball remembers the measles he had the year before.

Yes. Believe me. That's how it is. Take care. Good-bye. And let there be no more wars.

A MEETING AFTER THE WAR

[Note: The town Kralupy was heavily damaged in an Allied air raid in March 1945 (see poems on pages 123–135). Seifert used to go to Kralupy often as a child. He revisited the badly damaged town after the end of the war, in 1945. About to return to Prague, he waited for his train on the railway station platform.]

I had walked back and forth several times when an unknown woman suddenly stepped in front of me. Her smile alone was enough to make me stop.

"You don't remember me any more?" I looked at her face, which was still obviously beautiful, but marked by suffering and by the passage of time.

I blurted out: "Elsa!"

She gave me both her hands happily.

"You are so good to recognize me. My acquaintances don't recognize me any more. I knew you right away. So perhaps I haven't aged quite so much after all."

It was Elsa, Elsie. In Kralupy there had been many Jewish families before the war, especially among the merchants, and Elsa came from one of those families.

"Imagine, of all my Kralupy family, I am the only one who survived. Now I am waiting here for my cousin from Canada, who asked me to move there. And I am going to go. Everything here hurts me. I feel desperate here."

Elsa was one of the most beautiful girls in Kralupy. I had known her ever since I was small, but mostly only by sight. I had only talked with her two or three times, and then had merely said some unconsidered passing words. I always blushed shyly. She lived near us. I was taken with her. I would greet her bashfully and she would thank me with a smile. That was all. She was two or three years younger than I, and I would never have dared to be the first speak. It was always she who would stop me. She was beautiful. She was so strikingly beautiful that even women looked around at her. Perhaps she was not so conceited and proud as she seemed at first glance, but her walk was proud. My aunt used to say she walked like the queen of France. Of course I didn't know which one she meant. She also carried her pretty head so it seemed as if she despised other people.

Elsa took my arm intimately and began excitedly and hurriedly to tell me the dark tragedy of her entire family.

Her father and mother died quickly one after the other, four years before, in Terezín. She and her two brothers were dragged off to Auschwitz. Her husband was arrested soon after their wedding and died in Mauthausen, where they had forced him to carry heavy rocks up high steps. Both brothers died in the gas chambers. It was her turn, too, but when the Germans were preparing to flee before the Red Army, she and a few other woeful Jewish women managed to flee, gradually making their way home, following the Red Army. After the liberation their apartment in Kralupy, which the Germans had plundered, was occupied by several families whose houses had been destroyed. She was staying in Kralupy with some people she knew. There was nothing left for her except to go abroad. She could not live here. And she did not want to. She assured me again how happy she was that I had recognized her.

We walked together along the platform, and she asked me to talk to her about Kralupy, where she had been happy, young, and carefree. When I mentioned that she used to be beautiful and how much everybody was taken with her, first she smiled and then she started to cry.

A little later the train came on which I was leaving for Prague and her relative was arriving. When she smiled, her dark, deep eyes sparkled the way they used to in the old days.

Dante says through the mouth of the beautiful, but desperate Francesca da Rimini in the fifth canto of his *Inferno*:

> There is no greater pain
> Than to remember happy times
> In a time of misfortune.

Those are well known, often repeated lines. But, no, Dante was not right.

The train for Prague remained for about twenty minutes in Kralupy. There was no free track. However, I didn't see Elsa again. Snow started to fall from the dark sky: first big clusters, then smaller ones, but thicker and thicker. A violent snowstorm started. The dark platform vanished first, then the whole railway station, and finally all of Kralupy with all its wounds, sorrows, and sufferings.

Good-bye!

Many years later I started translating Solomon's *Song of Songs*. When I was looking for words for the speeches of love, the young, lovable face of Elsa from Kralupy appeared before me. It emerged out of the depth of several millennia, it came right up to me, and I said to her the lines of the unknown Jewish poet:

You are like a lily among blades of grass. Your figure is like a palmtree, your breasts are like clusters of grapes. Your eyes shine like doves in the shadow of a veil. Arise, my love, my beauty, come. Winter is gone, the time of singing has begun, the voice of the turtle dove is heard. Your lap is a garden of pomegranates and in it are rare fruits, henna and nard. Your lips are bedewed with honey, under your tongue is honey and milk.

I sat in the waiting train looking out the window, and saw nothing but the blizzard. I stared out the window attentively and fixedly, but I saw nothing except falling snowflakes. I watched them falling quickly, and reflected how many kinds of human kisses there are in this beautiful, sad world. All the kinds of kisses that love invents when a man's face comes near a woman's. And what of women?

There is the first kiss and the last kiss. But why start this sad song about love?

There are passionate kisses, when lovers almost pull their tongues out by the roots. And there are also kisses of love when passion sublimates itself into tenderness. There are long, moist, seething kisses, when human breath is like an invisible flower touching both the face and the nostrils.

But there are kisses which recall the palm of a hand held out by a beggar, and there are kisses which are like a coin dropped into that palm.

There are completely desperate kisses, but let us not talk about them.

There are also kisses in which lips kiss the heart of a woman. They have the effect of an injection into the heart. They stimulate an indolent heart and awaken one which is still asleep. Since I am speaking of a woman's body, there are still other kisses, too. Oh, God!

There are kisses full of smiles and joy. Kisses full of desire and also kisses of its fulfilment.

There are kisses without love and without warmth. They hardly touch the skin. Only custom dictates those, nothing else. There are sweet kisses and bitter kisses.

I do not count Judas's kiss.

No, one cannot add up the sum total. Nor can one add all the flakes I saw through the small window of a railroad car.

Then the signal sounded and the train started slowly towards Prague.

AN INTERVIEW ABOUT THE ART OF WRITING

("To Write with Black Ink on Black Paper," a conversation with František Hrubín)

HRUBÍN: People say you are writing your memoirs. I look forward to them more than to anything else. What is your attitude towards that kind of literature?

SEIFERT: Like everybody, I drag all sorts of shadows behind me, on a long piece of string. One of them smiles at me, another calls me names, still another feels ashamed and keeps silent. Some I should like to kick down into the precipice of oblivion, others I'd like to hold close to my heart. But they all clutch one another tightly, one cannot tear them apart. All of them call to me loudly, but I am not going to write my memoirs, partly because my memory is questionable. I did not write a diary, I did not keep any documents. The texts of my quite numerous lectures, I tear into little scraps of paper as soon as I have bowed to the audience, and throw them from a bridge into the first sewer or river I come to. After my lectures, I used to have a persistent feeling of shame. The spoken word flies away, but the text stays. So away with it!

However, so that I should not be suspected of wanting to wipe out of existence various unpleasant things which might bear witness against me, I finally decided that I would write twenty or thirty fairly long letters to my friends and acquaintances. According to need and circumstances, I would clarify various things in the past, confess my errors and mistaken opinions, and also, by remembering the dead around and behind me, I would add something to their portraits, which are so quickly forgotten. There would be enough such obligations. In life there come times when we prefer the literature of fact to the most attractive fiction. To put it crudely, we get fed up with fiction, but never with poetry; we need poetry to the end of our days. Therefore we like to reach for books of reminiscences.

HRUBÍN: . . .What did Karel Teige mean to you and to your generation in general? We younger ones passed him by, he was only a myth for us.

SEIFERT: I loved Karel Teige. I see it more clearly now than at the time. Hardly a day passed when we did not meet. He was a genuinely kind person, unselfseeking, friendly, brilliantly knowledgeable in matters of art. And quite unbribable. The things that

180

person knew! When we drew Vancura into our company, the conversations in Vancura's presence took on still greater height and depth, and they opened the world of the mind for me.

In those days, the shop windows at Topic and the bookshelves at Borovy used to be full of foreign books. Teige bought this and that. Immediately afterwards, he improvised translations in the Slavia coffeehouse over black coffee.

*   *   *

One day we were pacing along the banks of the Seine together . . . Teige passed by the Louvre with contempt. Nothing in there was of interest to us. I saw the Louvre by myself, later. But we went through all the galleries dealing in modern paintings.

We would spend hours sitting in the chairs of streetside cafés, and we did not skip one circus or wax museum. That was in keeping with our new artistic program, according to which art ceased to be art; Malevich with his famous square had ended the evolution of art. And poetism began.

What did Teige mean to us? A lot. When we were invited to give lectures in Bohemia and Moravia, it was Teige who gave us advice, formulated precise definitions, dictated passages which had to be accurate. Discipline was quite severe in those days. He was an unusually happy stylist. He wrote readily and quickly. He used to say he learned to do that when he wrote the Czech compositions for half his class in school.

He was the first and last authority in matters of poetry, art, and architecture.

*   *   *

It was Karel Čapek who invited the poetry of Apollinaire to come to Prague. But Karel Teige welcomed it and made sure it liked it here.

Professor Dominois, who used to stay in Prague for long periods, would say that a professor of French in Paris was not as well informed about modern French art as a secondary school student in Prague. This was Teige's doing.

When his work was silenced here, I never doubted that it must come back. It has happened already. I am happy that I have lived to see the day.

*   *   *

People write about the generation of the twenties as Wolker's generation. That is not quite correct. Rather it was Teige who determined the characteristic cast of this generation across the board — from poetry to the plastic arts, and to architecture. As far as our group of lyrical poets is concerned, it was Josef Hora who stood at its head, willy nilly, from the start. You can believe me. He affected it strongly. First there was proletarian poetry. Hora had an influence even on Wolker. At that time even Teige was discovering and propagandizing proletarian poetry, until poets, including Hora, began to abandon proletarian themes and Teige began to formulate the new program of poetism. It was a time of seeking new forms and making efforts to create them. Although later Hora moved in a slightly different direction, still his influence did not come to an end.

*   *   *

The time of this "poet of the soul" [Hora] will return. He has enough time, he can wait, if one thinks about his potential influence on future poets. His poetry is always present. Its beauty was never extinguished by the years.

HRUBÍN: "Open the door to the reader; it is his business to find his way inside." Léon-Paul Fargue said something like that. What do you say to the view which we hear now and then that the reader doesn't matter at all, that the poet can leave him standing in front of a closed door?

SEIFERT: I think of F.X. Šalda. Unfortunately I cannot remember right now where it is that he writes about the mission and place of a poet in the nation and measures him partly according to the power of his influence on the masses of readers. He values him according to the size of the interest which his voice arouses. Let us not overestimate the depth of the cultured stratum in the nation. At the same time of course we should not belittle the creative efforts of those who, perhaps obstinately, are attempting a new form today and are conquering new territories for their works. The first echoes of Vančura's books among the readers were not at all loud. I accept Teige's idea that only one kind of poetry exists, and that is inevitably revolutionary poetry. Neruda too was a revolutionary poet. . . . No development, even if it is followed by only a brief and narrow column of readers, will be without significance for the development of poetry. The criterion of quality is decisive even in the present time, of course. But I am saying obvious things.

So what does the modern mean in poetry? I think it is always that which in its new form resonates with the new reality which we are experiencing at the time, and so it attempts to embrace it, move it, change it. And only with the tools peculiar to poetry. Once somebody stated the aphorism, "Propagandistic poetry is good when it is good." That doesn't mean, of course, that poetry should be only propagandistic, even though I believe that at the right moment it has an immense strength. Think of [Wolker's] *Silesian Songs*! Victor Shklovsky once said about the propagandistic abuse of poetry, "One can hammer a nail with a samovar, but why do it with a samovar?"

The masses of readers, as we know, are rather inclined to conservatism and to the familiar comforts of old forms. So the poet often fails to meet his readers, or even conflicts with them. Without condescension, without concessions, he must again and again attempt to persuade the reader. How could he turn away from readers when his work can live only through them? There is no point to writing with black ink on black paper for the fleeting clouds.

I think that, with one small change, we could extend Russell's definition of human history to poetry, too. The history of poetry is also the history of great creators, those who create their works against the will of the wide masses of readers. But they always do so for the sake of the poetry of the future — if, of course, it is possible to win the readers over for the new ideas, with untiring effort. No work ever conquered everybody, that is self-evident. But it is equally certain that if a reader remains forever in front of a closed door, it is not his fault. The work is superfluous and bad. Every poet wants to be heard, even the most exclusive one.

I am in favour of poetry being engaged, if of course the writer has complete freedom. The affairs of the people and of the nation cannot be indifferent to any poet, especially a poet of a small and threatened nation like ours. Being engaged of course does not mean saying "Yes, yes" to everything. Poetry is a dialogue about truth, and it should be a passionate, entrancing dialogue.

* * *

HRUBÍN: Can you say what Šalda meant to the poets, how his influence manifested itself in poetry, in what poets were writing?

SEIFERT: Šalda's affection for the generation of the twenties never meant idyllic friendship and toasts in a wine cellar, as some people think ... Šalda always firmly defended his right and the right of every personality to develop according to its own inner laws, to grow and to become regenerated. That is how it happened that he found himself nearer to our generation, which was further removed from him chronologically than Čapek's generation. But, as is known, this involved some scratches, which Šalda's pen left on the faces of his victims.

He could not be bribed with smiles or with praise. Love and devotion to his person did not buy his approval. His presence was to us the highest determining authority, even though there are not and never have been authorities in history who did not have the right to make mistakes and even to commit an occasional injustice. Perfect people do not exist. This was something different. We admired his inexhaustibly rich personality, his mastery of Czech and world literature, we revered his genius which encompassed the past and the present. One could not fail to take to heart his knowledge and his teaching.

The example of his moral personality also impressed us. He never failed to take up every opportunity to wage a passionate battle. He worked and fought his way through to a position which possessed a certain aristocratic and spiritual dignity.

His private life was also exemplary. He was a marvellous human being.

He was unassuming and simple, but everybody gladly humbled himself before his beautiful and noble face which embodied leadership. He was democratic, but not without aristocratic manners. We believed in him. And what is most important — he taught us something. Today we look with a certain pity at young authors who look helplessly around the world of literature and find nobody to weigh their books justly.

He was a human being who loved beautiful humanity and knew how to laugh beautifully, the way every free human being convinced of truth laughs.

GLOSSARY OF NAMES AND PLACES

APOLLINAIRE, Guillaume (1880-1918), a son of a Polish mother and Italian father, came to France in his youth, served in the French Army in World War I and was wounded in 1916. An innovative poet, defender of the Cubists. Seifert translated several of his works.

BEZRUČ, Petr (1867-1958), pseudonym of Vladislav Vašek, famous above all for his one collection of lyrical poems, *Silesian Songs* (1909).

BIEBL, Konstantin (1898-1951), poet, committed suicide during Stalinist times.

BRETON, André (1896-1966), leading French surrealist, stressing dreams, the unconscious, and details of ordinary life.

CANAL de Malabaila (1745-1826), founded the "Canal Gardens" (or Canal Park) in 1790, in the Vinohrady part of Prague. It was a botanical garden which also served experimental scientific purposes. It is now part of the Rieger Park.

ČAPEK, Karel (1890-1938), Czech playwright, novelist, journalist, one of the outstanding men of letters of the First Republic; author of the *Insect Play* and *R.U.R.*

CENDRARS, Blaise (1887-1961), French poet, essayist, who used violent images and syncopated language; influenced Seifert.

CHOTEK GARDENS, a park near Hradčany in Prague, named for the Czech nobleman who as governor of Bohemia developed the area.

CLAM-GALLAS palace, in Prague, built between 1713 and 1719 by Fischer von Erlach; with a famous portal of Caryatid-Titans by Mathias Braun; an outstanding example of Prague Baroque architecture.

CLEMENTINUM, a group of baroque buildings from the 17th and 18th centuries; at the Charles Bridge, on the right bank of the Vltava (Moldau). The Clementinum used to house the philosophical department of Charles University, but now serves as the Czechoslovak State Library.

COCTEAU, Jean (1895-1963), a French poet, artist and film-maker.

DEVĚTSIL, a Czech literary movement and organization.

DE VIGNY, Alfred (1797-1863), French Romantic poet.

DOMINOIS, Fuscien (1888-1938), French Professor of Czech in Paris, who spent several years in Czechoslovakia.

DUBÍ, a town near Teplice in Bohemia.

EFFENBERGER, Vratislav (1923-), a Prague theoretician and critic, who wrote on Surrealism.

FARGUE, Léon-Paul (1876-1947), French Symbolist poet, a "walker through Paris," poet of musical language, verbal fantasies.

FUČÍK, Julius (1903-1943), a Communist writer, journalist, executed by the Germans.

GAVARNI, Paul (1804-1866), French illustrator, caricaturist.

185

GIRGAL, Ota, a Czech publisher.

GRANDMOTHER'S VALLEY, the grandmother of Božena Němcová used to live there. See Němcová below.

HALAS, František (1901-1949), great Czech poet, friend of Seifert.

HAŠEK, Jaroslav (1883-1923), author of *The Adventures of the Good Soldier Švejk* (1921-23), a comic, colloquial, irreverent antimilitaristic book of countless stories, available in the excellent English translation by Sir Cecil Parrott; the book is a witty classic to some Czechs and tasteless blasphemy to others.

HOLAN, Vladimír (1905-1980), an outstanding Czech poet, close friend of Seifert, after whose death Seifert wrote his poem, "Homage to Vladimir Holan".

HORA, Josef (1892-1945), outstanding lyrical poet, friend of Seifert; edited a supplement to *Právo lidu (People's Rights)*, the Social Democratic newspaper.

HOŘEJŠÍ, Jindřich (1886-1941), poet who studied in France and lived there for nine years; translated fifty volumes of French literature.

HRUBÍN, František (1910-1971), Czech poet, translator, playwright, journalist.

JACOB, Max (1876-1944), Parisian avant-garde poet, convert to Catholicism, arrested and killed by the Germans in 1944 because of his Jewish origins.

JESENSKÁ, Milena (1896-1944), Czech journalist, one of Franz Kafka's loves, wife of modernist architect Jaromír Krejčar, died in German concentration camp Ravensbrueck.

JEWISH CEMETERY, a famous cemetery in the former ghetto of Prague. Old tombstones, some dating from the Renaissance days, are crowded on top of one another within its walls.

JUNE, a Czech magazine edited by S.K. Neumann.

KAMPA, an island in the Vltava (Moldau) river, in Prague, a place of quiet lanes, old palaces, rich in historical atmosphere.

KARLŠTEJN, a castle south of Prague, founded in 1348 by King Charles IV of Bohemia (and Holy Roman Emperor), to be the site of the official residence of the Emperor and the treasury of the Empire's crown jewels.

KONOPIŠTĚ Castle, a mansion dating from the 13th and 14th centuries; the site of a large park, east of Prague.

KOŠÍŘE, a neighbourhood in Prague.

KRALUPY, a town on the Vltava (Moldau) river, near Mělník, where Seifert used to visit in his youth. In the 20th century Kralupy became an industrial centre. The oil refineries were bombed by Allied aircraft in 1945, with considerable damage to the town.

KRUŠNÉ HORY, mountains rich in ores forming the northwest border between Bohemia and Germany; steep on the Czech side; with many spas, watering places — Teplice, Jáchymov, Dubí, and others.

LITTLE TOWN, a section of Prague on the left bank of the Vltava (Moldau) river, nestling under Hradčany Castle, with small streets, steep alleyways, and old houses and palaces; the subject of stories by

Neruda, Czech 19th century writer. (Also sometimes translated as Little City or Little Side.)

LORI, see SOMKOVÁ.

MÁCHA, Karel Hynek (1810-1836), the outstanding Czech poet of the Romantic period, whose dramatic poem *Máj* (*May*) (1836) is his best known work.

MALEVICH, Kazimir (1878-1935), Russian Suprematist painter.

MARAT, Jean Paul (1743-1793), leader of the French Revolution, stabbed to death by Charlotte Corday on July 13, 1793.

MARINETTI, Filippo Tommaso (1876-1944), Italian poet, born in Alexandria, Egypt, initiated the Futurist movement in Italian literature.

MASARYK, Thomas Garrigue (1850-1937), the chief founder of the Czechoslovak Republic, President from 1918 to 1935. He was the incarnation of its spirit of liberal democracy, national independence, and alliance with France and England. He died on September 14, 1937, a time when the threat from Hitler's Germany was becoming ominous. Masaryk's death was deeply mourned by the population.

MORSTADT, Vincenc (1802-1875), Czech painter and graphic artist, known for his detailed views of Czech towns, which have as much documentary as artistic value.

MOZART, Wolfgang Amadeus (1756-1791), had many friends in Prague; visited Prague three times; he wrote *Don Giovanni* for Prague, and its premiere took place in 1787 in the Stavovské Theatre (see Glossary below) in Prague. Mozart is associated in many ways with the city of Prague and Bohemia. He died neglected and poor and was buried in the pauper's grave in Vienna; the site of his tomb is unknown.

MUCHA, Alphons (1860-1939), Czech *art nouveau* painter and illustrator, moved to Paris, became famous for his posters (for Sarah Bernhardt and other theatrical personages as well as for commercial establishments).

NÁCHOD, an old town in eastern Bohemia, with a Renaissance mansion and park.

NĚMCOVÁ, Božena (1820-1862), the author of *Grandmother* (1855) a Czech prose classic, spent her youth at Ratibořice near Česká Skála and Chvalkovice; her grandmother, the subject of her book, lived at these places in Bohemia in her youth.

NĚMEC, František (1902-1963), a friend of Seifert's, who wrote lyrical poetry, and later became an outstanding author of newspaper stories based on courtroom cases.

NERUDA, Jan (1834-1891), Czech poet and author of stories of life in the alleys and old houses of the Little Town in Prague. Seifert edited a volume of his works.

NEUMANN, Stanislav Kostka (1875-1947), outstanding Czech Communist poet.

NEZVAL, Vítězslav (1900-1958), member of *Devětsil* from 1922 onward, Surrealist poet, translator.

OLD TOWN SQUARE, had a column (with a Virgin Mary and Angels) which was sometimes regarded by some Czechs, who had won independence from Austria-Hungary, as a symbol of the old monarchy.

OLŠANY, a Prague neighbourhood famous for its large cemetery.

PETŘÍN, a hill in Prague, with an observation tower and funicular railway (restored into service in 1985), and covered with parks and gardens.

PEOPLE'S HOUSE, a building on Hybernská Street in Prague which was the centre of Social Democratic activities and also lodged the printing plant of *Právo lidu* (People's Rights), the newspaper of that political party.

PÍŠA, Antonín Matěj (1902-1966), poet, writer for various Social Democratic newspapers, friend of Wolker. After 1925, wrote only literary criticism and reviews, and edited numerous works by others, including Seifert.

RATIBOŘICE, see Božena Němcová.

REVERDY, Pierre (1889-1960), French author of free verse and prose poetry, collaborator of Apollinaire and Jacob.

RIMBAUD, Arthur (1854-1891), French poet, precocious genius, completed his poetic work when he was nineteen, travelled adventurously in exotic lands from the time he was twenty till his death.

ROYAL PAVILION, also called Belvedere, a Renaissance building with a fine colonnade in which an early form of racquet tennis used to be played; near Hradčany, in Prague.

ROYAL ROAD, the traditional route taken by the procession during the coronation ceremony of the Czech kings, from the Týn Cathedral in the Old Town Square, through the streets of the Old Town, across Charles Bridge, and up through the streets of the Little Town, towards the Castle and St Vitus' Cathedral at the top of Hradčany.

ROŽMITÁL, a 14th century castle in Central Bohemia, near the town of Příbram.

RUDOLF II (1552-1612), Hapsburg King of Bohemia; under his rule the Prague Castle (Hradčany) became a centre of astronomy, alchemy, art, mysticism.

RYBA, Jan Jakub (1765-1815), Czech composer, cantor in Rožmitál, composed a Czech folk Christmas mass.

ST VITUS' Cathedral, a Gothic church, was started in the 14th century, adjoining the Royal (later Presidential) Palace on the mountain of Hradčany; it dominates the skyline of Prague. The Cathedral of St Vitus contains a side chapel consecrated to St Wenceslas and is strikingly adorned with large precious stones.

ST WENCESLAS, the patron saint of the Czech nation, was the Ruler of Bohemia, killed by his brother's soldiers in 929, or a little later. A medieval hymn to St Wenceslas, imploring him to intercede with God on behalf of the Czech nation, is part of the common heritage of the Czechs, and arouses great emotion among them, particularly in difficult times. St Wenceslas' crown, ornamented with large semi-precious stones, dates from the eleventh century, rebuilt in the 14th century and it is a part of the Czech Kings' coronation jewels.

ŠALDA, F.X. (1867-1937), journalist, editor, critic, professor of Romance

Literature at Charles University, editor and chief author of *Šalduv Zápisník (Šalda's Notebooks)*, a periodical of independent literary opinion in the 1930s.

SÁZAVA, river south of Prague.

SHKLOVSKY, Victor (1893-1985), Russian literary critic, leader of the 'Formalist' School of literary theory, also author of many novels.

SHULAMITE, the beautiful woman addressed in Solomon's "Song of Songs".

ŠÍMA, Josef (1891-1971), Czech Surrealist painter and graphic artist, who moved to Paris in 1921; painted mythological landscapes.

SOMKOVÁ, Eleonora, known as Lori (1817-1891), met the poet Mácha when she was seventeen, as an amateur actress. She was his fiancée when he died on November 7, 1836, two days before the date set for their wedding.

STAVOVSKÉ Theatre, built in Prague in 1783 as the National Theatre. Became in 1797 the Estates Theatre (belonging to the Estates of Bohemia). In 1787 the premiere of Mozart's *Don Giovanni* took place in it.

SUK, Ivan (1901-1958), a classmate of Seifert's, who wrote verse and later courtroom reports — a well defined and popular journalistic-literary genre in Czechoslovakia.

TEIGE, Karel (1900-1951), theoretician of art and literature; a loyal supporter of the Communist Party, he came into conflict with it in the 1930s over the trials held in the USSR and the cultural policy of the Czech Communist Party; after that, ostracized and isolated.

TEREZÍN, formerly a Hapsburg fortress, north of Prague on the Elbe River, which the Germans in World War II turned into a concentration camp, by evacuating the population and replacing it with inmates, for the most part Czech Jews. About 35,000 prisoners died there by May 1945; many more passed through in transit to their deaths in other extermination camps.

THUN-HOHENSTEIN, an Austrian noble family which had branches in the Czech lands since the 17th century, and was prominent in Czech and Prague administrative affairs in the 19th century.

TOYEN (1902-1980), the name assumed by Marie Černínková, Czech painter, illustrator, graphic artist, who moved to Paris.

TZARA, Tristan (1896-1963), Rumanian poet, founder of Dada movement in literature and art.

VANČURA, Vladislav (1891-1942), outstanding novelist, writer of flamboyant poetic rhythmic prose, arrested and shot by the Germans during World War II.

VILDRAC, Charles (1882-1971), French poet.

VLADISLAV, Jan (1923-), Czech poet, translator, resides in Paris.

VONDRÁČEK, František, a well-known psychiatrist in Prague.

VRCHLICKÝ, Jaroslav (1853-1912), one of the leading Czech poets of the nineteenth century. Seifert edited his works.

VYŠEHRAD, a hill in Prague overlooking the Vltava (Moldau), site of ancient castle church and Hall of Fame.

189

WHITE MOUNTAIN, at the outskirts of Prague, the site of a disastrous battle which the Czech and Moravian Protestant units lost to the Austrian Catholic army, in 1620, marking the beginning of three hundred years of Hapsburg rule.

WOLKER, Jiří (1900-1924), author of markedly proletarian poems, with Communist ideology.

ŽIŽKOV, proletarian part of Prague, where Seifert was born and lived as a boy.

NOTES TO INTRODUCTION

1 Quoted in Jaroslav Seifert, *Ještě jednou jaro*/Spring Once More/,
   Prague, 1961, by Jiří Brabec, "Dokumentární pásmo o životě a
   díle"/Documentary Materials about [Seifert's] Life and Works/.
2 See p.151 for the passage in his memoirs in which he speaks of his
   feelings for his father and mother.
3 See p.155
4 Several passages are indebted to the fine critical observations in an
   essay by Křetoslav Chratík, published as a postface to an
   anthology of Seifert's poems in the Czech original, *Ruce Venusiy*
   (*Venus' Hands*), Toronto, 1984, pp. 283-297.
5 Reminiscences by Milan Kundera.
6 Translated from the French text in *Le Monde*, Dec. 11, 1984.

NOTES TO POEMS

"Prague"
The foolish emperor; see "Rudolf II" in Glossary.

"Spanish Vineyards"
In the late 1930s, news of the Spanish Civil War was followed with great interest in Central Europe. Leftist Czech intellectuals and artists sympathized with the Government and against the Franco side.

"To Prague"
The poem refers to the liberation of Prague in May 1945. Reminiscences, p.171.

"Sometimes We Are Tied Down"
Jewish cemetery, see Glossary of places.

"Song of the Sweepings"
Rorate — A hymn prayer sung as part of the early morning mass during Advent.

"St George's Basilica"
Romanesque church, older than St Vitus' Cathedral, which adjoins it. See also Glossary for St Vitus' Cathedral.

"Prologue"
Phrygian cap — adopted during the French First Republic as a symbol of libertarian or revolutionary sympathies.

"The Canal Garden"
See Glossary under Canal de Malabaila.

"The Plague Column"
In Catholic countries it was a custom for columns to be erected in public places as an expression of gratitude for having been delivered from the Plague (or Black Death) which devastated various countries. The columns were usually dedicated to the Virgin Mary and were later regarded by Protestants or anti-Austrian partisans in Czechoslovakia as symbols of Catholic and Austro-Hungarian ideology. Some of them were torn down after the Czechoslovak Republic was set up in 1918. A column was set up in Old Town Square after the Swedish (Protestant) attack on Prague was repelled in 1648. A figure of The Virgin Mary and four angels crowned the column. The column was wrecked by Czechs on November 3, 1918 (Seifert watched the event himself).

Little City = Little Town, see Glossary.

"Lunar Ironmongery"
Little City = Little Town; see Glossary.

"View from Charles Bridge"
Marian song — songs of devotion to the Virgin Mary, associated with Baroque, Counter-Reformation times.

Royal Road — see Glossary.

"On his Parents":
1 The titles of the excerpts from Seifert's reminiscences are the editor's. The translations were made from Jaroslav Seifert, *Všecky krásy světa* (All the Beauties of the World), Toronto, 1981.

"How I Became a Poet":
1 Translated from the text in Jaroslav Seifert, *Ještě jednou jaro* (*Spring Once More*), Prague, 1961, ed. by František Hrubín and Jiři Brabec.
2 Soon after the episode described, Seifert published his first book of poems, *Town in Tears*.

"Publication of His Third Book:
1 The original lines by the Czech Romantic poet Macha read, "Light laughter on the face/Deep sorrow in the heart."

"A Few Minutes Before Execution: May 1945":
1 A ritual performed before executions of noblemen in Tsarist Russia to indicate their being deprived of their status before their deaths.
2 People's House, see Glossary.
3 Negotiations — The German General Toussaint was ready to surrender to leaders of the Czech Uprising, but his superior general refused to do so. The leaders of the several Czech revolutionary organizations, which had formed a coordinating Revolutionary Committee, finally, on May 8, negotiated an agreement under which the German Armies were permitted to withdraw westward in order to reach and surrender to the United States armies west and south of Prague.
    The Germans gave up all weapons except sidearms. The first unit of the Soviet Army reached Prague at 6 a.m. on May 9.